If I Could Paint the Moon Black

Imbi Peebo's Wartime Journey

from Estonia to America

Nancy Burke

BookLoc

Saint Petersburg,

D0905871

Published by BookLocker.com, Inc., St. Petersburg, Florida.

Printed on acid-free paper.

BookLocker.com, Inc.
2019

First Edition

ADVANCE PRAISE FOR "IF I COULD PAINT THE MOON BLACK"

"Imbi's story, written by Nancy Burke in great detail, gives the reader a deeper understanding of the impact World War II and the Soviet and Nazi Germany occupations had on Estonians. The book is a valuable addition to the literature that has appeared since the collapse of the Soviet Union."

-- Ilvi Joe-Cannon, co-editor of *Carrying Linda's Stones: An Anthology of Estonian Women's Life Stories*

"There are so many statistics I could cite that would illustrate the brutality endured by people living under occupations by both Hitler and Stalin. Imbi Peebo's story, written by her friend Nancy Burke, cuts right through the clutter of history's recorded facts, to reveal a very human story of survival under those dark circumstances. While Imbi is not alone in that experience, her story represents tens of thousands more people...all whose stories deserve to be heard. This is a good place to begin to listen."

-- James Tusty, co-filmmaker of "The Singing Revolution" and "To Breathe As One".

Nancy Burke offers a significant contribution to the literature of eye-witness accounts with her beautifully written story of Imbi Peebo Truumees' life as an Estonian child refugee during World War II. Burke writes Imbi's story with great care and suspense that strikes a perfect balance between descriptions of place and event, childhood pleasures and overwhelming fears. The reality of what happened in during the war years can only really be glimpsed through those who lived through it and understood their experiences. Imbi is a brave and perceptive person, and Burke gives her the justice she deserves.

--Alice Elliott Dark, Professor of English and Creative Writing, Rutgers' Newark MFA in Creative Writing Program, author of *Think of England, In the Gloaming,* and *Naked to the Waist*

While the larger world needs to remember such stories as the one I have written here, I dedicate this book to the grandchildren of Imbi Peebo Truumees, for whom I believe this story is most important. HEILI TRUUMEES, MARKUS TRUUMEES, LILLY AASMAA and MIKK AASMAA

Table of Contents

Introduction

The history books recorded the war crimes of the German Nazis. What the history books do not tell is the impact the invasions and takeovers by both the German and Soviet regimes had on the everyday lives of the Estonian people. The Soviet Union was an ally with the USA, Britain and France. Stalin's crimes were hidden and, perhaps because of the magnitude of horror the world experienced upon discovery of Hitler's killing, the world did not turn its attention to Stalin's crimes until Russian dissidents like Aleksandr Solzhenitsyn (who smuggled his work out of the USSR in 1968) and Andrei Sakharov (the nuclear physicist who was sentenced to exile in 1980 for his criticism of the USSR's human rights abuses) saw their work received in the west.

Stalin and his government and his army were responsible for the deaths of 50 million people -Ukrainian, Belarus, Russians, citizens of the Baltic states of Estonia, Latvia and Lithuania and other lands overrun and incorporated into the Soviet Union. Dissidents and citizens were shot if they leaked information to the western press. This may explain why the public of the western world did not learn the extent of the Soviet's oppression until much later. And, at the end of the war, when Estonia was again the Soviet Republic of Estonia, the occupying Soviet government repressed all information that did not serve the best interests of their state.

It took forty-seven years for the second occupation of Estonia by the Soviets to come to an end. Families like Imbi's, in exile in the United States and elsewhere, feared going public with their personal stories while the Soviets still controlled their country. Imbi's grandmother, Olga, stepmother Elsa, half-brother, Taavet, uncles and cousins remained in Estonia under Soviet rule. The danger to them, if her story or anyone else's story of repression and exile went public, was very real. Now it can be told.

I met Imbi Truumees after attending the first New York screening of the film "The Singing Revolution" at the invitation of Ilmar Vanderer, my neighbor whose foundation had funded the completion of this documentary by James Trusty about the restoration of Estonian independent rule over their country in 1991 after forty-seven years of Soviet occupation.

After the screening, Imbi and three other Estonians who were children in 1945 told the stories of their families' escapes into Germany ahead of the Soviet taking of their country at the conclusion of World War II. I was so impressed with Imbi's story and her spirit I approached her at the end and introduced myself. I am a writer, I said. I would love to write your story. This was in October, 2008. She and I met and *became close friends while she elaborated upon the details of her and her mother's experiences as refugees. Imbi told me stories she had never shared with her children, had never spoken of in many years. This was an extraordinary experience for me. My study of Eastern Europe had occurred during my undergraduate years as an anthropology major at Montclair State University. Dean of the School of Social Sciences, Philip Cohen, taught a class, "The Peoples of the Soviet Union" which introduced me to the fifteen republics under the USSR.*

In 2008, I was an author in search of an inspiring story to write for my next book. That day at the screening, I found that story and a strong and intelligent central character. This book is the result of Imbi's telling and my recording of her experiences. It is a work that I hope will serve as a memoir so her grandchildren will know of her courage. It is also an important part of oral history finally recorded in writing after decades of silence about oppression and hard labor and the threat of murder by Stalin and his regime. There are countless stories similar to this one. Imbi asked me once why I approached her and not the others after that screening back in 2008. "It was you, Imbi. It was your spirit, your courage and the fact that you took responsibility for your mother at such a young age." This story is dedicated to Lydia Vahter, to Grandmother Olga, to Rudolf Peebo and, of course, to Imbi for whom this project was an unexpected pleasure in her grandmother years. I thank her for entrusting me with this very important work.

-Nancy Burke
2014

CENTRAL CHARACTERS

Olga Vahter, Imbi's grandmother

Olga's Children
> Leonhard (wife Maanja)
> Erich (wife Pouli)
> Eevald
> Ellen (husband Julius)
> Lydia Vahter, Imbi's mother
> Artur
> Karli

Imbi's cousins
> Virve
> Renate
> Toivo
> Eldor

Rudolf Peebo, Imbi's father
> Elsa, Rudolf's second wife
> Taavet, their son

Kaaritas, Grandmother Olga's sister's grandchild and
> Imbi's friend at the farm
Amanda, Lydia's friend who hid her from the Russians
Aino, Imbi's friend in Narva
Helene, Maanja Vahter's sister
Marie Peebo, Rudolf's mother and Imbi's grandmother
Oskar, Rudolf's brother
Hans and Oskar, German soldiers at the hospital

If I Could Paint the Moon Black

Imbi Peebo's Wartime Journey

from Estonia to America

PART I

Viivikond to Lauriveski

Grandmother Olga's farm at Mahu.
The ladder leads to the hayloft where the children slept.

CHAPTER 1

I remember that morning in June 1941 when the trains came to the station in Vaivara near Viivikond, where my mother taught and I attended school, Imbi began, recalling the events of more than 70 years ago which had forced her to escape from her native country, leaving behind relatives, possessions and memories in order to survive.

Grandmother Olga and I stared at the cars steaming with fresh hay early in the morning, long before any news of their real purpose reached us. I remember thinking, "there are no cows in Vaivara. Why are there cattle cars in the station?" Soon I would realize the horror of what was happening right in front of us.

Our citizens were being taken directly from their homes during the night, places of work, or right off the street and loaded up into train cars, never to be seen again. We went to the train station not only because we were curious. We carried food with us and tried handing it through the slatted cars to those on board. Grandmother didn't tell me why there were people in those cars or why they needed our food, but I followed her lead and helped her. I didn't see whole faces, just eyes, but mainly I saw hands poking through the slats, some taking food, others handing notes to strangers to take to family members.

Our police captain in Viivikond told us he saw the family of the mayor rounded up and sent aboard the first of the cars in the first train. Grandmother and I watched as whole families, neighbors we'd known well, whose children went to my mother's school, climbed aboard under the watchful eye of the brown uniformed soldiers. There were separate cars for the men, the women and the children. We saw families divided up, children eventually even taken from their mothers. And the soldiers glared at those of us who were not ushered onto a car.

"Nyet!" the soldiers shouted at us as we approached the cars with food and water. "Russian," whispered Grandmother Olga.

"It might be a good idea for you to not be home, in case they come knocking on the door," Viivikond's police captain had hurriedly told Mother while Grandmother and I were out, which explained why she was suddenly home from school in midmorning. "They are taking the educated ones."

I am thankful for every day that I am here. Imbi paused after sharing the first of her many life-changing memories, and I looked up from my scribbling as she and I sat in the living room of the home her husband, Arvid, built with his own hands in Cresskill, New Jersey.

There were days, months really when it looked like we might not survive. The very first day of the Soviet takeover, I realized, and I was only nine years old, that I needed to take my father's words very seriously. I must be in charge, for my own sake, for my mother's sake. That simple statement made me strong and it probably helped save my life and my mother's life more than once.

As I listen to this, I hear Imbi with the innocence of a child as she recalls her childhood. I also hear Imbi, the mature woman, a grandmother, and an accomplished scientist whose career in the United States was as remarkable as her years of flight in Estonia, Poland and Germany. And, inevitably, I hear her reflection on the history of World War II and its impact on the personal lives of so many courageous people and particularly the Vahter family and the Peebo family (her father's), Imbi's relatives who each faced variations of oppression whether they stayed in Estonia or fled.

I was born in 1932 in Rakvere. Estonia was an independent country at that time, since we had won our freedom from the Soviets in 1918.

Estonia is a small country of 1.2 million people just to the west of the Narva River, which separates it from Russia. To the south is Latvia, to the west, the Baltic Sea and Poland, and the Gulf of Finland borders the northern edge of the country. The language is related to Estonia's northern neighbor, Finland.

Estonia's history is one of continual takeovers by larger, stronger nations, but since it is such a tiny country, not much is written about it in the history books that most Americans read through our school years. Nor did many documentaries of World War II tell of the fate of the citizens of the Baltic States that lie between Poland and Russia. A long history of occupation culminated in a victory for the Estonian people who, in 1918 won their independence and established themselves as a republic. This is the Estonia into which Imbi was born, in 1932, but things soon changed.

In 1939, the Soviet foreign minister Vyacheslav Molotov and the German foreign minister Joachim von Ribbentrop signed the Molotov-Ribbentrop agreement, a non-aggression agreement wherein they agreed not to invade each other's territories. In this agreement, Hitler and Stalin agreed to divide up the lands between Germany and the Soviet Union, including Poland, Estonia, Latvia and Lithuania. As a result of this agreement, the Soviet Union annexed Estonia and in June, 1940, Soviets began their systematic take-over of the country. Deportations of Estonian citizens began in June 1941. That is when Imbi's innocent childhood ended and a long and difficult journey began.

My parents had divorced when I was five years old. It was just my mother and me most of the time, Imbi recalled. I saw my father and spent many happy moments of my early years at his house with his new wife and their new baby, Taavet, but for the most part, I lived with my mother.

Mother was a school teacher in Sillamäe, then later, a principal in Viivikond, a tiny settlement, and our apartment was attached to the schoolhouse, as it was in most settlements at that time in Estonia.

"You are in charge, Imbi," my father told me during one of my visits with him just after their divorce. He too was a principal of an elementary school, in Varangu, and he lived on in the apartment that had been our home for my first five years of life. "You are the head of the household. You are in charge of your mother." Imbi paused and I looked up from my scribbling. "An odd thing for my father to tell me," she said. "He always told me that and from the very beginning, I took his words very seriously." I wrote this in my notebook with a question mark. "Maybe he wanted you to feel important?"

"Yes, I suppose," Imbi said. "But at five years old?" She laughed. "It is good that he said that. It stayed with me. Ask Arvid. He knows who's in charge!"

"She is," Arvid laughs. "Imbi is maybe five feet two inches tall, but what she lacks in size she makes up in sheer force. I know who's in charge."

Imbi's husband of many years, Arvid Truumees, is a tall man with a deep voice and his own story to tell. He was evacuated by the Germans with his family from Saaremaa and followed a different path to the United States. Imbi and he met after they arrived. Arvid is also a walking encyclopedia of Europe during and after World War II and often helped with this project by supplying history lessons and digging up maps and photographs.

At seventy-seven years old, when she and I began this project, Imbi was not slowing down, and she is a gracious host. On the coffee table is a spread of crackers and small pieces of bread and a spinach dip, some slices of cheese and the glass of water she carried to me. A wall of windows with a view of the wooded backyard let a stream of bright sunlight into her contemporary home. We sat in comfortable chairs, me with notebook in hand, and had spent a few minutes getting acquainted. We discussed the recently released documentary film "The Singing Revolution," which tells the dramatic story of how Estonia's successful efforts to regain independence in 1991 resulted in the collapse of the Soviet Union, and the freedom that her people in exile now feel to discuss their pasts. "My children always tell me to write this all down," she says. "I tell them, when I retire I will." She laughs. "Arvid and I are so busy all the time, we'll never retire."

Rudolf, Lydia, and Imbi

When she and Arvid are not traveling the world, she helps her daughter at least once a week. Sirike is an internist so Imbi helps at her office handling paperwork and billing. On school holidays, Imbi's grandchildren are often her responsibility, something she takes great pleasure in doing for her family. And, holidays are always at her home for her son and daughter and their children.

The separation of my parents was a mystery to me. Imbi continued to recall her childhood. As a young child, I remember happy times. I don't remember arguments between them. It wasn't until my father introduced me to his new wife, Elsa, when I was around eight years old, that I began to understand why my mother and I no longer lived with my father. Looking back, my mother was not a practical person. She was artistic in her nature and very intelligent. She worked hard in her job as a school principal. Her name was Lydia. As a young woman, she attended Teachers' Seminary in Rakvere and trained to be a teacher. Her other talent was in designing clothing, which she did for herself and for me. The clothes she fashioned were just beautiful. She was a perfectionist, with every stitch straight, every seam finished, every style modeled after the pictures she saw in magazines or newspapers. She was the best-dressed woman in Sillamäe, Viivikond or Narva or anywhere in between, even during the bombings.

As I contemplated Imbi's description of Lydia, I wished she were still alive and could answer Imbi's questions and mine, which grow in number as we meet. We were inseparable, my mother and I. Arvid knew when he married me he was getting both of us.

Grandmother Olga

My mother and I spent the school year in Sillamäe, then later in Viivikond. At age five it was impossible for me to be in charge, of course, so my Grandmother Olga took care of me while Mother worked. In summer we moved to Lauriveski, three kilometers from Mahu beach near the Gulf of Finland to the north. There my mother's sister Ellen and brother Erich lived in adjacent small houses with their families. They each owned a small farm and raised some cattle, sheep and chickens. It was a quiet and naturally beautiful place. My grandfather died three months before I was born. He was a blacksmith on an estate named Kalvi, owned by a German baron. There were many such estates in Estonia in the old days. There my grandmother learned to speak German quite well. Grandmother and I cleaned together, we cooked; we walked together to the market. Mother did the sewing and that was enough with her duties at the school.

I really had an unusual childhood. I didn't have a home, not really. I know how important that is to children. It is something taken for granted, but I don't. And, of course, she takes a break from her narrative to ask me about my family, my home. And I do. Imbi's story is also about her extended family. Grandmother Olga was the mother of five boys and two girls, Leonhard, Erich, Eevald, Artur, Karli, Ellen and Lydia. Imbi tells me bits of their stories as well as her own, the danger, the starvation they faced, the means by which they were able to save their own lives and the lives of others, much of which she knew nothing about until long after she began her new life in the United States. This is her story as she told it to me.

CHAPTER 2

"They are taking the educated ones," Mother repeated.

Once she shared this with Grandmother and me, we wasted no time. Mother and I packed two small satchels and the three of us walked into the forest that surrounded Viivikond, hand in hand. Mother took us with her this first time she went into hiding. Of course she would. I distinctly remembered I was responsible for her as much as Grandmother Olga was responsible for me.

I knew this forest from days of playing among the pines with other children. Tall trees, a soft bed of needles underfoot, filtering sunlight from the blue dome of sky. It was cloudless on this June day. There were others in the woods too. Stepping quietly so as to not make noise or to draw attention to our presence, we walked together, stopping for short rests here and there, vigilant for any sign of uniformed men. We found a place to spend the night. There we were, under a starlit sky, with a bed of pine needles and a very small basket of fruit, some water and a bit of bread. I slept. I don't know if mother did or not but at daybreak she had the appearance she had most mornings just after being awakened for work, hair mussed, a wrinkle along her cheek from using her bag as a pillow.

"How long will we hide?" I asked her.

"I don't know," she said. "Until we know something. Until they're gone, I suppose."

"Then will we be safe?" I asked, feeling unsafe and certain we would remain so.

"I don't know," she replied. But, later that day, after she left Grandmother and me for what felt like days but was only a few terrifying hours during which I imagined the worst, she learned somehow, mysteriously, that the trains had left Vaivara and so we returned cautiously to our school and our home, but not for long.

"They came for you last night," a neighbor said. "They knocked on your door. There were three of them. Then they came to mine. I told them a lie. I told them I had no idea where you were." We saw tire tracks in the dirt on the road near our apartment and schoolhouse, boot prints too.

Then Grandmother let out a short laugh. "Well, the truth is you didn't know where we were." Grandmother Olga kissed the top of my head. She did that often as a way to reassure me as we received news she knew she would have to explain to me later. The neighbor, I wish I could remember her name, told us who else had been escorted to the trains. All young, all educated, and yes, they'd taken the children with them.

Imbi sat in her living room with me and I saw her eyes draw away from the window she'd been gazing toward as she recalled these details for me. I remember that glance exchanged between Mother and Grandmother at that moment. I knew that I would not be accompanying my mother, wherever she was going next. She would never risk my being taken with her even when her own life was endangered. I cried. And, I imagined my father being disappointed in me if I let her go off without me. Imbi laughed. Then she said with a somber look, "I wouldn't be able to protect my mother from them but she couldn't protect me if we were together."

"We'll go to the farm," Grandmother Olga said. "Imbi will be safe there."

My mother simply nodded. "And I'll go into the woods. That is where the resistance will form. The Estonians always go into the forests." She looked at me. "Imbi, someday you'll know what I'm saying." She looked at Grandmother. "I'll get word to you somehow." She kissed us both good-bye.

The long trains with those cars for cattle were gone for now, but could easily return. And so Grandmother Olga and I left Viivikond and mother for the farm. We never returned to Viivikond. Mother never taught school there again. Mother packed a small bag and went back into hiding. I watched what she took. The clothes she'd made for herself, the fancy ones, modeled after the magazine pages, stayed in her wardrobe. She took only the clothes she wore when we did chores. She was, before my eyes, becoming less the impractical mother my father put me in charge of. She looked solemn and resolute. Still, when she hugged and kissed me, turned and headed out again with her small case and a sack with whatever food we could fit inside, I remember feeling like I was letting my father down, letting go of my duty to take care of her. I did not know if I would ever see her again.

Grandmother Olga and I boarded a train, a westbound train, and I recalled her saying earlier, "East, the cattle cars are heading east," and asked her where the eastbound trains would stop.

"Russia," she said. "It is a very large country. Who knows how far they will take them."

We didn't understand the magnitude, that day in June, of this rounding up of people. I only knew my mother was at risk and I didn't know when I'd see her again, if ever. We know now that in a matter of four days, an estimated 10,000 Estonians were deported on those trains to Russian labor camps in Siberia.

CHAPTER 3

Grandmother Olga and I arrived at Lauriveski, near Mahu, three kilometers from the Gulf of Finland. We were earlier than usual this summer and Aunt Ellen and Uncle Julius, Uncle Erich and his wife Pouli all knew why without my telling them although, I filled them in on every detail of that overnight stay in the woods.

"Cattle cars took the people," I said. "They came for Mother but we hid."

"You, Imbi," Uncle Julius used to say to me, "we knew if there was anything to know, you would tell us." Imbi explained to me, "I used to follow him around all day while he did his chores. He used to tease me that I would talk him to death."

"Four hundred and nine cattle cars crossed the border," Uncle Erich announced. "From Russia. The border reported six full trains have returned to Russia."

Uncle Erich and wife Pouli

"So they are not finished," Aunt Ellen said. She was at the stove, turning breakfast sausages in a black pan on the first morning I awoke at the farm without Mother. The scent as they sizzled had wafted to the hayloft where my older cousins and I slept. We had dressed quickly

Aunt Ellen with husband Julius

and run to her kitchen. Now, we sat at her long table and watched Grandma Olga dip into a bucket of fresh milk for each of us. We sipped while we waited. Pancakes would follow the sausages.

"Have we heard from Mother?" I asked Grandma Olga.

"No," Grandma Olga answered. "But we will. We should soon."

Erich, my uncle, who placed a piece of bread on the plate in front of me asked, "Have we heard from Karli, or Artur?"

Artur, my mother's brother, was a graduate of the conservatory of music in Tallinn. He was living in Narva at this time, near Uncle Leonhard who practiced law in Narva, and he had taken a job teaching music at an elementary school there. At the advice of Uncle Leonhard, Uncle Erich told us, Artur had fled to

Tallinn upon the arrival of the Soviets. He would try to get on a westbound train to avoid being taken into the Soviet army.

Karli, the youngest brother in my mother's family had gone to the maritime college and worked on ships in Tallinn. Not a word from him either.

"Not a word," replied Uncle Erich.

Aunt Ellen lifted sausages onto a wide platter and handed it to Uncle Erich who sat at the table with a cup of coffee in his hand. He helped himself and passed it along. "It will take some time, I'm sure."

Grandma Olga stared at Aunt Ellen, then at Uncle Erich. "The educated ones," she stated. A long moment of silence hung itself there among us. The platter reached me and I took a sausage and passed it along. I knew what she meant. Among my aunts and uncles, only those present had not attended university.

"But going to university makes you smart," I said. "They are all too smart to let someone take them."

"Yes," Aunt Ellen said. "Imbi's right. And my brothers know how to take care of themselves. Let's eat. There is much to be done today." She dropped a spoonful of lard on her skillet. It sizzled. She ladled batter and spread it in perfect circles. I knew they had to turn brown before she flipped them and handed them over, one at a time, to whoever had their plate in the air when she turned. Soon all of us would be fed. My mouth watered for them. While she cooked, she assigned work.

I was the youngest of the cousins. And, since I wasn't there all year, I didn't have the chores my elder cousins had. Every morning there were cows to milk, chickens to feed, a garden to weed, and of course, cooking and washing and all sorts of jobs for everyone.

"Imbi, you will go with Grandma to the garden and pull weeds. Eldor, the new potato field needs a plow. Toivo, you can gather the eggs and milk both cows. Uncle Julius is tending to the pigs, and he's fixing a roof tile in the hayloft. Toivo got wet from rain two nights past. We can't have that all summer. Lunch on the second cabbage field at noon. Listen for my bell and meet me there." She sat, finally taking the last of the pancakes for herself. She lifted her fork. "Whatever happens, we've still got the day's work. If I hear anything, I'll send Imbi to spread the word."

I lifted my chin and studied her while she chewed her first mouthful. She was beautiful, my mother's sister, with her rounded cheekbones above a long delicate jaw and chin. Her eyes, simple and intelligent, were on her food and then her children, the same blue as Mother. Aunt Ellen was suited for farm life, not like Mother whose hands did not easily crack eggs, break open pumpkins, throw seeds, or wring the neck of a chicken.

Aunt Ellen sang as she did all these things, her mind, I imagined, filled with sounds and melodies. They welled up in her all day. Why did she not go to the conservatory like Artur? Her soprano could carry across three fields to call us home to supper. She, like mother, had been divorced once. Uncle Julius was her second husband. A kind man, tall, a bit gaunt compared to Uncle Erich's stout bearing, and jolly in a perfect harmony with his wife's way of stepping through rugged farm life as though it were all a dance, and all it needed was her music to lift it above the mundane. She left music in her wake as a plow leaves dust, sparkling in sunlight and conjuring magical imaginings of spirits unseen but there nonetheless.

Later, after Grandma and I weeded, Aunt Ellen instructed Kaaritas and me to go wash the dirt off ourselves before lunch. Kaaritas was my grandmother's sister Lonni's grandchild who lived across the road and was the same age as me. She'd gotten word I'd arrived and helped us in the garden. The river ran through both farms and that's where we bathed. In those days, it was deep and cool. A platform of wood was constructed as a place for us to bathe. Now, she carried a bar of soap to share. We held our breaths and submerged ourselves, the cold constricting my chest just for a second until I relaxed. It was mid-June and the sun was high and warm. I could hide here, I imagined. If only I could hold my breath for longer. I could stay under if they came to take me. I blew slow bubbles, exhaling to prolong my stay. Nobody would think to look here. My lungs threatened to burst so I lifted my head above the surface and inhaled. Kaaritas splashed me, handed me the bar of soap and I quickly made lather and rubbed myself from head to foot. Back and forth with the soap, we scrubbed each other's heads and made a game. One, two, three, under. I shook my hair, came up, did it again, until the surface of the water showed clouds of translucent suds and a rainbow gently moved downstream spreading out, diluting itself until, again, we were in pristine water. Mother could hide here with me. Could she hold her breath long enough? She and I swam together during other summers when she and I spent weeks at Narva Jõesuu, where the Narva River meets the Gulf of Finland.

There were many things I did not know about Mother. Now that she was not here with me, and I did not know where she was, it was suddenly important to recall what I did know. She grew up here, on this farm, where Kaaritas was now busy doing the same. Mother had attended the Teachers' Seminary, which told me she was smart; that's why she was a teacher, and that is how she met my father. I knew she would have to find someone who could protect her, now that she and I were separated. What was her favorite color? What size shoe did she wear? Mama's last words, "It is better if you don't know where I am. So that if someone asks, you can honestly say you don't know," were in my ears, telling me she was far more practical than Father had described.

I felt movement under the arch of my foot, there on the river's bottom. "Crayfish!" I shouted at Kaaritas.

"Where?" she cried. She gulped air and went under. I followed. She reached low and lifted a rock. Two scurried for shelter a few feet away and Kaaritas grasped for them. They were quick, but she was quicker. Her second try was successful and she stood, river water running off her face, hand held above her in triumph. "Got it!" she cried.

"We need a pail," I said.

"Here," she handed me the struggling crayfish, brown and gray, its claws grasping, reaching but missing my fingers by fractions of centimeters. Kaaritas leaped up the riverbank toward the house and disappeared. My shoulders, above the water line, had begun to shiver. I lowered myself, clutching the crayfish and holding it aloft, until my shivering stopped. She was back quickly and filled the bucket with water. I dropped our first catch in with a plunk.

Back in the river, Kaaritas lifted a rock just as my hands took up a position of captor. Exposed, the poor crayfish did not have a chance. I was quick. I knew just where to grab so each set of pinching claws could not fight me. Kaaritas only knew we were having fun together and that later we would relish our catch. I knew those things too, but I felt a new sympathy for the crayfish even while we filled one bucket, then went back to the house to find another. Kaaritas and I meant to drop them into a steaming pot and watch them turn red, crack their claws and suck the meat from inside.

By noon, my chest hurt on every inhale. Kaaritas's lips were purple. The buckets were swarming with our captives. We dried ourselves, our fingers wrinkled, the skin under our fingernails and toes blue like our lips. We carried our catch to the kitchen where Grandma Olga set a pot to boiling on the stove. One by one, Kaaritas and I dropped our catch into the churning heat. When they were red they were cooked through. Grandma Olga lifted them with tongs and set them in one of Aunt Ellen's crockery bowls. We drank the warm tea Grandma Olga brewed when she saw our pale white skin and blue veined extremities and the goose bumps on my arms. We spent the next hour picking the tender white meat from those crayfish, savoring each sweet morsel, made all the more precious by the scant size of each piece we were able to pull from the claws, suck out of the legs and break from the tails. We had no need for Aunt Ellen's packed lunch served out in the cabbage fields to the rest of the family, but when we heard her song and her bell, we lifted what was left in the bowl and carried it to the rest of the family.

A week passed. Then another. The sun passed the solstice point in late June and set only for a few hours each night. The water grew warmer. Kaaritas and I bathed in the river and eventually left the crayfish alone, letting the population replenish itself and grow fat while we found other diversions. The farm had plenty. Uncle Julius was more than pleased to have our company as he did his work even though I overheard him tell Aunt Ellen he was seriously expecting that I would talk him to death.

I lined up with my elder cousins each morning, waiting for Aunt to assign chores. My favorite was picking wild strawberries in the woods under the small pine trees. Kaaritas and I used the stems of their ferns to string the tiny sweet-smelling strawberries as though they were pearls. After filling about a dozen strips, we walked home where Grandma Olga made jam of the ones we did not steal for immediate consumption. I prayed silently for word from Mother, and when I remembered, for Uncle Artur and Uncle Karli. When chores did not distract me, I returned to the second step near Aunt's front door, facing the road, watching for her, imagining she was just about to round the curve and come into view. She would, or, someone, anyone, might bring a letter, a rumor, a reassuring word. Where was she? Was she safe? Had she hidden herself well enough? Could she be on one of those cattle cars, heading east, to Russia? Was she alone? I kept quiet rather than ask Grandmother Olga the question that was continually at the front of my mind. I knew if she heard anything, I would be the first person she would tell.

CHAPTER 4

I loved the labor of the farm. Of course, being so young, I didn't work as hard as my cousins, but I stepped in to prove myself at harvest time by raking the cut rye into piles which were then made into bundles to dry in the sun. I worked alongside my cousins Renate, Virve, Toivo and Eldor, all of whom were five to eight years older than me. We used huge rakes to gather the hay. I remember tossing the hay onto huge mounds once it dried. This was feed for the animals. And some was stored above the tiny houses we lived in, in the loft where my cousins and I slept. We worked hard, then Aunt Ellen brought us bread and butter and cucumbers and we would eat sitting on a large blanket out in the fields.

Grandma Olga had offered to share her bedroom at the side of the small house, but I wanted to sleep in the hayloft with my cousins. This was also Mother's usual place when she joined us most summers. I didn't want to miss the fun that was part of that communal sleep in the hay. The loft was a wide area above the house where Uncle Erich stored hay for the horses for the winter months. Eldor and Toivo might have preferred that I not be there, but I insisted. The sweet drying hay was several feet deep and had the most wonderful smell.

Cousin Renate

The sun beat on the roof all day so even after sundown, when cool air gently blew across us from the windows, comforting warmth rose from just below. We had no beds, just blankets spread over the hay.

Privacy was not something the small house afforded anyone in the family, (except perhaps during a trip to the outhouse or a cleansing sauna down near the river). It was clear after a few nights that Eldor and Toivo, who were teenage boys, would prefer to sleep without the companionship of their visiting cousin. Their spots were side by side on the west side of the wide-open space. The girl cousins, Renate and Virve, slept a few feet across toward the east. My place was lined up just next to Virve's on the girls' side. After we all prepared for bed and settled in, and the sun was still high in the sky, discouraging us from sleep, someone would start a song, or a game, or a story, and it did not matter how old I was, I could listen, sing along, or take a turn telling a story of my own.

One evening after dinner I heard Toivo whisper "Kalvi" to Eldor. His look suggested mischief and secrecy. Uncle Julius had just told me he was heading out to lead the horses back to the stable after dinner. He had become accustomed to me trailing after him in this nightly task. I stood up to follow him when I again caught that word, "Kalvi" exchanged between Eldor and Toivo. That glint in their eyes meant fun. I was not going to miss out on any fun.

I said, "Uncle Julius, my legs are tired. I think I'll stay here."

Off he went, whistling and digging in his pocket for a hard candy.

I attached myself to Toivo when he took a bar of soap and a towel and headed toward the river to

Cousin Virve

bathe. Halfway there, he turned to me, "Imbi," he said, "would you please let me go to the river alone?" I did not know about boys becoming men and their changes. It took Toivo's pleading with Grandma Olga, to please keep me near the house, to peel me off him. Off he went.

Cousin Toivo

There was Eldor, sweeping the porch for Aunt Ellen. "What is Kalvi?" I asked. He smiled the way he always did when I approached, as though my presence was mildly amusing. Then he frowned. He stopped sweeping. "Where did you hear that, little one?" he asked.

"You know," I said. "Toivo just whispered it to you. What is it?"

"It is nothing," he said. "Go help Grandma dry the dishes." He resumed his sweeping.

"Can I help?" I asked. I reached for his broom.

"You want to sweep?" he asked. He handed it to me. "Imbi, what a pest you are. Everything I do, you want to do, unless it's the hard work." He left me there on the porch. I dropped the broom and followed him.

"But Eldor," I said. "Kalvi is something. I know you know. Tell me." I paused, then I said, "Or, I can go ask Aunt Ellen what it means."

Eldor stopped and turned. "No," he said. "Aunt Ellen will not know what it means." After a short pause, he continued, "If I tell you, do you promise not to say a word to my mother, or Grandma, or Uncle Erich, or my father?"

I put my hand up in a silent pledge.

The sun did its slow slide into the distant pines, but long before it disappeared, my cousins all had their eyes shut. Toivo had taken a long time at the river and sauna and returned looking pink and scrubbed. He said he was tired. I watched as he combed his hair. It was bedtime and he combed his hair. That gave me a clue. The girls too, had taken special care, brushing their hair before they settled into the hay, eyes closed, flat on their backs. They never slept on their backs. Usually when I awoke at night they were curled around blankets, pillows tucked under their ears. Tonight, they lay like planks, rigid torsos flat against their blankets, arms along the sides, mouths closed. There were no stories or songs before bed.

Eldor had told me what Kalvi meant. It was a manor, he said. It lay just north of Aseri, toward the sea and had been home to rich German landowners for centuries. He did not tell me why Toivo and he had exchanged the word like it was secret.

I lay down, prepared to sleep along with my cousins, but the sun in the southwest still sent light through the window. It hit my closed eyes and beckoned me to stay up. The birds were still singing in the trees. Without the usual voices of my cousins, talking and singing, they were so loud. Sleep was impossible. I sat up.

"I have a story," I said. "Once in a small village..."

"Shh," hissed Virve. "I'm trying to sleep."

"This is a new one. I haven't told you before," I started again.

"Imbi, we're tired. Please lie down and go to sleep," Toivo said.

"Then why," I asked, "did you comb your hair? So you would look handsome in your dreams?" I laughed at him.

"Imbi," he said. "You play all day. We work and we're tired. Please go to sleep. Or, just lie down and pretend so it's quiet for us."

I lay back on my pillow and pulled my blanket up and around me. I stared at the ceiling. I sat back up. "I milked one of the cows today. I helped Grandma Olga pull weeds. I picked strawberries, but I'm not tired."

"Imbi," said Renate. "If I sing a song for you, a lullaby, will you at least try to go to sleep?"

"A song!" I said. "Yes, sing "Ema, Kallis Ema." (Mother, dear mother) That's one of my favorites."

She sat up and sang while I lay back down, flat on my back like the rest of them. Her voice was soft, almost a whisper, like Aunt Ellen's, high and sweet and, with this lullaby, soothing. I rolled to my side and she stroked my back gently. She pushed my hair from my forehead. I closed my eyes, imagining for just a moment it was my mother singing me to sleep. I no longer heard the birds. It was as though they listened too and were lulled to sleep as I was. She sang another, and another. Slowly, I drifted off, not aware when her singing stopped or that the evening's long and silent shadows enveloped us in its prolonged summer twilight.

There was movement in the room. I sat up, startled. Were they here to take me? Had the soldiers found me? Was it Mother? No. It was Toivo. He was standing in the hay, shoving one leg into a pair of trousers.

I heard the rustle of fabric. The girls were in dresses. I watched Virve help Renate tie a ribbon in her hair. Eldor sat tying his shoe. I stood up and reached for my clothes hanging on the wall hook over my bed.

"Where are we going?" I asked. "What happened?"

By the light, it was late, but certainly it was not morning yet. I hurried to dress. I stood, pulling my nightshirt over my head and dropping it on the hay. Virve bent to pick it up.

"Imbi," she said. "Nothing happened. Everything is fine. We're just going out for a walk." She handed me my nightshirt.

"Well," I said. "I'm coming too." I eyed her dress. It was one Mother sewed for her last summer. It was not a dress for walking. It was a dress for a party, or for church going, or for dancing.

"Kalvi," I said. "You're going to Kalvi."

She looked over at Eldor for help in what I knew was a lie. A walk? In the middle of the night?

Eldor said nothing. He just studied me. He studied Renate. He exchanged glances with Toivo.

Toivo said, "Little pest." He sat to pull on a pair of socks.

"I'm coming with you," I said. My resolve was all the stronger now that I understood the magnitude of their attempted deception. Tired from working all day! Renate's singing had almost worked. I looked at Toivo. He had bumped and made the noise that woke me.

"Imbi," said Eldor. "You can't come. It's too far for you to walk. You will never keep up with us on your bicycle. And," he came over and sat on my bed, pulling me into his lap. "The dance is not for little girls. It's for grownups, or Jugendlicher." He used the German word.

"I want to come," I said. "I've never seen a manor. I want to see Kalvi." I said it in German so he would know he could not exclude me. I could keep up with him in anything. It didn't matter that I was nine and he was almost sixteen.

"No," Toivo said. "Go back to bed." He turned to the girls. "We're wasting time."

I watched the girls and Toivo turn to step carefully down the ladder. One by one, their heads disappeared from view. Eldor lifted me off his lap.

I jumped and ran toward the ladder, turned and scrambled down after them. I was not dressed and my shoes were buried somewhere in the hay.

My fear upon awakening had not completely left me even though I knew there were no soldiers here to drag me away. Perhaps my raised hopes that Mother had arrived, dashed to nothing so instantly, hurt more than I knew. Maybe their earlier attempt at deception cut more deeply than it might have any other summer, when I knew the world was safe and Mother was near. Maybe the hay itself frightened me, the image of those cattle cars, loaded with it, mingled with everything else in a forgotten dream just before Toivo's bump woke me. Their departing backs were so much like Mother's when I last saw her. I only knew I would not let them leave me alone.

"I'll tell Aunt Ellen if you don't take me with you." I was halfway down the ladder; Toivo was halfway across the yard when I said it. Eldor was above me in the loft. Their silence told me I had won.

"Imbi," Eldor said. "Come back up and put on some clothes."

Toivo looked at the sky. Virve crossed her arms and frowned. Renate sighed in defeat.

"Here," Renate said. "I'll put a ribbon in your hair." She pulled a small length from one of her braids. "Up," she said. "Up the ladder. Get your pretty dress and hurry."

Eldor stepped aside as I rushed past him. Renate climbed back up behind me.

"Here, wear this," she said. She held out my best skirt and blouse. I wasted no time and slid into my clothes while she found a clean pair of socks for me. I stood as still as I could, the excitement and relief mingling with my sweet sense of victory. Kalvi! I was to see the manor. Renate tied the ribbon around a lock of hair she pulled back from my forehead. It rested against the back of my head and I reached up to touch it.

"Leave it alone," she said. "You look pretty. Let's go. And you must be quiet until we reach the road." She turned to the others. "Let's hurry. The dancing will be over if we don't."

"Dancing?" I asked. "Is there dancing at Kalvi?"

"Shh," Toivo said. "Imbi, you'll spoil everything if Mama wakes up. Here, take my hand."

"Is there a girl there for you?" I asked Toivo. His pink skin flushed a deep red. Virve laughed. "Well, why then is he so polished up?" I asked. "There must be a girl there for him."

Toivo tugged at my hand. "If we don't hurry, she'll be gone before we get there."

I let him lead me. "What's her name?" I asked.

"I don't know," Toivo said. "I don't know if she is going to be there. There is someone for everyone, Imbi. Maybe my someone is already at the dance, dancing with someone else."

"You like girls?" I asked Toivo. He complained about me all the time. He had joked at breakfast about sticking a potato in my mouth to keep me quiet when I had what he called 'too many questions for such a little wisp of a thing'. He teased Renate. He argued with her. He laughed at her at chores. "You take three times as long as it takes me," he said, in the milk barn just this morning. "Squeeze harder, like this." He placed his larger hands over hers. He pulled. Edna, the cow, objected with a sideways kick. The bucket Renate had filled to halfway spilled. Edna chose that moment to relief herself. Renate leaped up from her stool and backed away.

21

Toivo fell backwards trying to avoid the stream of yellow urine. Renate and I laughed.

"Ah yes," Renate said. "Next time I will do it your way!"

Toivo couldn't help himself. He leaned on his elbows and laughed. "At least she didn't get me wet!" he said. That was Toivo, proud and bossy one minute, still a little boy the next.

"Imbi," he said. "I like girls, yes. But do me a favor and don't spread it around." He lifted me and placed me sideways on the bar of his bicycle. "Hold on." My legs dangled while I clutched the handlebars and balanced. Once we were out beyond the fence we picked up speed riding on the grass next to the road so the patches of mud would not splatter us.

We headed north, away from the shadows as night fell. The pines turned black as the sky became a blanket of gray. This was scrub pine country; the soil was red. I had heard there were streaks of blue clay in the cliffs further northwest of Aseri, long lines of sky blue in the layers of brown and red. It surprised me to see it on the road below us where rain from a storm three days ago had washed the topsoil away.

Toivo and I followed Virve and Renate. Eldor left us far behind. I knew Toivo wanted to catch him. "Go faster," I said. "I won't fall off."

Toivo laughed. "No, you want to sit down tomorrow and not have your bottom hurt." We hit a bump and he said, "See?"

The distance between Virve and Renate grew because Virve, I realized, was waiting for us.

"I'll take Imbi," she said "if you want to go on ahead."

"No," Toivo said. "She may be my date for the evening. Right, little pest?"

Virve sped off again after Renate. We were not that far behind, not really. I stopped thinking about being last and what that meant to Toivo when the first glimpse of electric lights from the castle flickered in the distance.

"Is that Kalvi?" I shouted. "That's it, isn't it?"

Toivo said, "That's it. What do you think?"

The road dipped and we picked up speed on the downhill.

Toivo said, "Hold on!"

We recovered easily enough and coasted past a line of carriages and wagons along the approach. The northern sky was navy blue. Kalvi estate's windows blazed against the stark backdrop. I counted four stories; every level had bright rectangles in neat rows. The road circled a fountain and led to the front door that had been flung wide open. Silhouettes moved in haste toward the door. Music spilled toward us, a tuba's bursts of deep tones, other, lighter tones floating along above it. A polka. Eldor had found a rack for bicycles and we pulled to an abrupt stop next to him. Virve checked her hair in a tiny mirror while Renate waited to use it next. I smoothed my skirt down along my legs. Toivo took one hand, Renate took my other and we followed Eldor inside.

Dancing girls and boys swirled past in a dizzying array of colorful dresses and swinging hair. Music, loud, energetic, pulsing and full of the promise of fun. But, not for me. I was the only child there. Everyone else was tall, adult or heading that way much sooner than me. Renate danced off with a friend. Virve stood next to me for a few minutes but soon she was gone too. Eldor next. Toivo was left standing there. I grabbed his hand. "Don't go," I said. "Please!" Everyone in the room was moving. Legs and skirts stepped past in a frenzy of energy. I could see nothing but bodies pressing past.

Toivo lifted me off the ground and held me high on his shoulders so I could see the dancers from above, not feel as though I'd be crushed any minute.

"What time is it over?" I asked.

"Why?" Toivo asked. "Don't you like to dance?"

I nodded. "I do, very much. Let's go." I danced with my cousins and their friends until three o'clock in the morning.

Toivo laughed. "Imbi," he said. "Did one of us say you were too young for this?"

I was too young, but that didn't stop me from dancing all night. I was having a glorious time, but I must say, being only nine and tiny, the swirling mass of teenagers left me feeling a bit worried that I'd overstepped my limits, but only because I was not ready to stay up as long as this great party lasted. To my great relief, finally the music stopped and my cousins gathered around me to prepare for the journey back to the farm. Toivo carried me on his back and somehow managed to push his bicycle at the same time, all the way back to the farm. He tried, at one point, to sit me on the bicycle seat and push it home, but I was too tired to sit on the handlebars as I had on the ride to Kalvi. The others rode and circled back to check on us. I have a memory of light in the sky by the time we reached the hayloft but I have no memory of climbing the ladder to my bed. I only remember waking up very late the next day. Toivo was my protector, and I promised I wouldn't tell anyone of our adventure in the middle of the night, so he and I, and of course all the others, never uttered a word.

A week later, again, in the middle of the night, I woke to find my cousins dressing and sneaking down the ladder. This time, I simply rolled over, tucked my head under my pillow and went back to sleep. I was happy I'd seen it once, but I never wanted to do it again, not at this age.

CHAPTER 5

It wasn't Mother who appeared on the road one day in late summer. It was my father on his bicycle. It was a mystery to me back then as to how we came to know things that happened far away from us. We had no telephones at that time; there was no television and very little was broadcast on the radio. Once the Soviets took over, they decided what to announce on the radio to the Estonian people and we learned early not to believe most of what they said. So much of it was in Russian anyway. So, how my father learned that I was already at Grandmother's farm and that my mother was hiding somewhere was not immediately clear to me. Nevertheless, here he was, on a bicycle. After my initial surprise and delight at sighting him I felt a sudden drag on my heart. Where was Mother? Did he come with bad news? I ran for Grandmother Olga and Aunt Ellen. But no, Father quickly shared his news of Mother. She was with Amanda, her long time friend. She was safe, he said with his eyes on mine. She was staying with Amanda somewhere along the coastline. She had sent word to him and told him I was here. He thought I might come stay with him and Elsa.

My father, Rudolf, was a school principal, like my mother, but in a different settlement, called, Varangu. This was about 104 kilometers from Viivikond but only 37 kilometers from Mahu. These three places formed a triangle that made up the early geography of my childhood. I became like a gypsy, moving from place to place. But, the family was close and loving and there was never a moment of disrespect between my divorced parents and family members on either side of my family.

And so, after he had a meal and a rest, and after I gathered up my clothes and gave hugs all around, my father set me on the bar of his bicycle and we left. Looking back, I imagine he thought I would be safer with him than at the farm. Later, I am sure he thought otherwise, but at this moment, I was so happy to see him at first I didn't notice how hard the bicycle bar was on my behind. It was a long distance from Mahu to Varangu and we didn't waste any time. The ride felt endless. What a relief it was when we arrived in Varangu. We entered the apartment that had been our home before Mother and I left for Sillamäe.

"Imbi," said Father, "this is your step-mother, Elsa."

I stared. I remember my first understanding right then of why Mother and I were on our own, why Father had given me responsibility for Mother. Here was another woman in her place. Elsa shifted her weight and moved the bundle of blanket with a hairy head protruding to her left arm and reached out to touch my hair with a gentle gesture of welcome.

"And who is this?" I asked and reached for little Taavet. He was three months old and very chubby. He reached for me and I took him, kissed his forehead and immediately became his second mother.

Elsa and Taavet

I was smitten with Taavet despite how heavy he was in my arms. My bottom still felt the pain of the bicycle bar but I felt like I was coming home again. I half expected to turn and see Mother in the kitchen cleaning up or at her sewing machine working away as she had in my earliest memories. But, no, it was Elsa who now ran this household for Father and Taavet.

His crib was in my old bedroom. I would sleep on a cot against the far wall of that room. But first, Elsa fed us.

There had been no trains with cattle cars in Varangu. Father and Elsa talked of their neighbors and Father's new trucks and most of all of Taavet, who sat in his infant chair and chewed his fat hand with a gleam of happiness in his eyes. They asked me so many questions about that day when the soldiers knocked on doors in Viivikond and came looking for Mother. And, they wanted to know of Mother's family on the farm. I shared as much as I could.

"Imbi," Father said. "You are still in charge, aren't you?"

I felt a bit of shame as I sat and tried to find an answer.

"You don't have a house of your own to be head of right now Imbi," he said. "But you are still head of the family. We all agree on that, don't we Elsa?"

My stepmother smiled and nodded. And with that, I felt relief. I was still important enough, home or no home, for him to remind me, in his favorite way, of my position in the family. Looking back, I am sure Father's purpose was to reassure me, a daughter of divorced parents was a rare species in 1941, of my place in the world and in the family, despite the fracture, and to remind me too, of the love between all of us.

After our long bicycle journey, I stayed with them and helped Elsa with my baby brother. I did not have as much to do when I lived with Father as I did when Mother and I were alone in Viivikond or with Grandmother at the farm. Here in Varangu I was a child again, with friends, with Father's parents' farm only a kilometer away. The Soviets were still in charge, but this settlement was tiny; it had not drawn attention from our occupiers, not yet. Mother was still in hiding. But, Father too was an educated man and under the surface tranquility, I knew what that meant. He was a smart businessman also. He and his brother Oskar were entrepreneurs. Several years earlier they bought a small truck and started a business for transporting goods between Estonia and Russia.

During this visit with my father, Uncle Oskar left Varangu with the truck as usual one early morning and headed toward the Russian border. My father never saw the truck or his brother again. We will never know if Uncle Oskar was sent to Siberia along with the countless others or if he was shot by the soldiers who took his truck. My father told me, several weeks later, through his bitterness and his tears, that the Soviet system does not allow individuals to own businesses. Uncle Oskar's truck and the goods he was carrying were now illegal and so were confiscated by the Russians. My father owned a second truck and an automobile and these, I learned later, along with his education, were enough to make him a target for arrest.

It was a Sunday morning in August, 1941. A car pulled up to the front of our house and five men in Russian uniforms stood up and turned toward our front door. I saw them first, through the window. From inside our apartment, visitors were visible through a glass door into a small foyer. I was in the living room when they approached. I could not pass the door and get to the kitchen where Elsa was preparing breakfast without risking being seen. I could not warn her. Father was visible through the glass door before I could tell him. I knew to hide. I knew Mother's instinct had been to hide. I also knew it was possible to hide, if you were smart enough. But, Father answered the door. Perhaps he was not fully awake, perhaps he did it so they would take him and not have to search the house for him and in so doing take us too. Perhaps he just was caught unaware. He never described that moment, or that decision, to me. I knew, if I could not warn Elsa, they could take her too. Most times they took the wife and family with the one they wanted. The mayor's family in Viivikond, the whole family, without suitcases, barely dressed, flashed before me. That could be us. I ducked toward the rear of the house. Taavet was still in his crib, still sleeping, wrapped in his blanket with a pattern of stars. I could be silent. I was. I gently closed the door to his nursery and opened the window. I pushed aside the curtains and went to him, praying he would not make a sound, lifting him slowly, carefully, willing him to stay asleep, to not cry out as I took charge. Voices, loud ones, shouting between my father and those men in Russian uniforms, reached me.

Taavet was a big boy. I lifted him to my shoulder, went to the window, lifted my legs over the sill and slid to the ground. The jolt of my landing woke him. "SHHHHH," I whispered. I ducked low and crawled along the edge of the house on two legs and one arm, clutching Taavet to me. Down along the fence, I could just fit through the opening toward the back of the yard. I praised Taavet. He clung to my neck. He made not a sound. My hand under his buttocks told me he needed a change of diaper. His body was not prepared for such an unusual morning. I dragged us through the fence and ran to the stand of trees where I would not be visible from the house, from the road, from a passing stranger. I hugged my baby brother close, whispered to calm him, pointed to a squirrel in a nearby tree. His eyes were barely open, sleepy, hungry, I'm sure. He let the squirrel distract him and pointed at another. I turned, leaned slightly around. Nobody was coming. Grandmother and Grandfather Peebo's farm, I thought. I will go there. Taavet and I will go there. Where was Elsa? Did they take Elsa too? I heard the thud, thud, thud, thud, as four car doors shut, the purr of the engine started, and my Father was gone. Elsa? Where is she? With Father? Would she see the open bedroom window? Would she follow? Would she stay to not draw attention to us? I waited a minute, two, feeling the weight of Taavet as he turned his fat little neck this way and that. I hoisted him higher on my hip and turned away from the house. I knew the way. I had run back and forth to Grandmother Marie's many afternoons, to surprise them, to gather vegetables to bring home to Elsa for dinner. It was just through a small woods, over up-heaved roots, fallen pine needles, twigs, fallen leaves of golden yellow, and thick blueberry bushes that were empty of fruit because I'd already picked most of it. I crossed a tiny stream on the boulders I had carefully arranged, when I had first arrived with Father. I never could imagine back then that a journey to Grandmother Marie's farm would be like this. A rock wobbled under my foot but I was quick and did not lose my balance. The far side of the water was wooded and a narrow path led me to the edge of the trees. I saw Grandmother's house in the distance. Smoke curled from the chimney as though this Sunday was like any other. Odd how I remember that now. Comfort and safety, I suppose, are never noticed until they are threatened. A twig snapped under my foot. Just one. Then silence. No, I breathed in, nobody was following me. I remembered Viivikond. They knock on doors. Sometimes they go into the woods. I ran. Taavet bounced against me, his chin slipping toward my shoulder. I hoisted him. His little hands clutched at my pigtail. I pressed him closer to my chest and passed through the final hundred meters across an open field to Grandmother Marie's back door.

A firm sound of the door in its frame, a shudder, then silence. In my mind I still heard them opening and closing the doors to that car. Thud, thud, thud, thud, and the engine turning on. I heard it again as Grandmother shut the door behind me. Thud, thud, thud, thud. My father was gone.

"He's arrested," I spoke in bursts of short shallow breaths. "Father. They took him." I paused. "I think Taavet needs a new diaper. Look." The blanket he was wrapped in was damp. So was the sleeve of my dress and all down the front of me.

Grandmother took Taavet from me. She said, "Imbi, sit down. Rest. Where is Elsa?"

"I don't know," I said, sitting on a stiff chair, my elbows on the kitchen table. "I waited, but I was afraid to wait too long. I don't know if she was taken with

Father, or if she hid, or if she went out the back door and was gone before me. I don't know." I looked up into her eyes. "Do you think she would come here?"

"I hope so," Grandmother said. Grandfather Gustav brought me a glass of milk and a slice of bread.

"Eat, Imbi," he said. "You're safe here. They don't want us. We're old. They will not come here."

"Would they follow me?" I asked. "Did you look?" I jumped up, ran to the window, and cried, "She's here! Elsa's here! She's safe." I ran to the door and swung it wide, hugging her as she arrived, her arms reaching around me, pulling me to her, tears in her eyes, streaming down her face in shiny streaks. "Oh, Imbi, you did it. You saved Taavet too! Where is my baby?" she reached for Taavet, wetness and all lifted him, pulling him to her, kissing his fat cheeks.

"They took Rudolf."

CHAPTER 6

They took him in a car, not a train. And they didn't take him far. Imbi learned of the cells in Haljala where he was held later. She learned about where they took the Estonian prisoners. It was not far from the apartment and schoolhouse. She also learned of the dead, the ones they shot immediately. Fate was on her father's side that terrifying August when the trains with the cattle cars were still at work, systematically targeting the ones the Soviets saw as threats or the men young enough to serve in their army. They used trucks in places that were too far from the railroads. Imbi's father spent a week in a cell awaiting either his death or transport to Siberia or perhaps he would have ended up a soldier in their army. Elsa, Taavet and Imbi returned to the apartment. If Father was released, or if anyone received word of him, they needed to be there where he could find them or so they could learn of his fate.

The German and Russian treaties at the end of World War I, particularly the Brest-Litovsk Treaty, which kept the Bolsheviks out of Estonia and the other Baltic countries, created a precedent in Estonia, a belief that Germany was the power most likely to assure an eventual restoration of Estonian independence. Germany had acted as a liberator in 1918 when Estonia became independent for the first time in hundreds of years. The Germans forced the Soviets to withdraw from Estonia in 1941, and so, with a renewed hope for independence, the Estonian people cheered and celebrated and welcomed them as liberators. For Imbi's father, they came just in time.

A few weeks after Father's arrest, the German's arrived. By now it was September, a year after the Soviets had swooped in. In his cell, in the basement of a building, all Imbi remembered him telling her was how he heard shots as the Soviets were ordered to shoot their prisoners before fleeing in the face of the advancing Germans. Father expected to be shot next, but they must have run out of time because he was left in a cell alone. The Soviets ran for their own lives ahead of the oncoming Germans. When the Estonian people ventured into that prison, they found Father with his hands and feet bound with barbed wire.

We were reunited a week later. He simply walked in our front door. His arms and legs were covered with cuts and sores and Elsa nursed his wounds and tried to get him to rest, but he had other plans.

"We are leaving...immediately," Father said. He'd been home less than an hour. Fleeing Soviet soldiers were everywhere and he knew he could be shot on sight by any of them. He must have seen enough on his journey through Haljala to know things he would never tell us.

Father built a bunker, a cave, into the side of the riverbank and we lived there, abandoning the schoolhouse, hiding from the fleeing Soviets, fearing that they would kill us as they retreated in front of the Germans who were moving across Estonia from the west. We could see them; the Soviets were still around. They were in retreat, but the fear that they would conscript Father and take him with them was just as real. They could not see us however; our bunker was well hidden and built in a series of bends in the riverbank. Our cave was dark and damp but we made do, not knowing how long we'd be there or where we might go to feel safe.

I remember peeking outside. Our bunker was dug into the wall of ground next to the river. Father had dug it with twists and turns. The tiny opening hid the labyrinthine tunnel where we stored what we could of the food we brought with us. There were no canned goods at that time. We had to make our food last. I remember smoked meat and fish, salted herring, bread but nothing fresh like fruit or vegetables which could spoil in the summer heat with no refrigeration. And, I remember conserving water. I don't remember how we managed without toilets, but we did. I do remember the fear that Taavet would cry and be heard outside. But, because the bunker was so twisted and full of turns underground, sound did not travel to the outside. One morning, I crept to the opening and peered out. Three Soviet soldiers were making a fast run, splashing across the river. I knew their uniforms. They were brown. There were other mornings when I saw others fleeing. There were no guns, no gunfire, no tanks or other machines of war. All I saw were fleeing Soviet soldiers. This lasted about a week, then the uniforms on the soldiers we saw were no longer Soviet drab but German green. We emerged to learn that our country was now occupied by the Germans.

As green replaced the drab brown of the Soviets, the Estonian people, including my family, emerged from hiding. The Germans came in large numbers, with tanks, and horses and trucks filled with men in uniforms. I watched in amazement as my people greeted the parades of invading Germans with applause, with bouquets of flowers, smiles and open arms.

It is difficult for the world to understand the hope and optimism we felt at the appearance of the Germans. For our family, it was liberation from a harsh occupier who threatened our lives. To the rest of the world, now, after the crimes of the German Waffen SS and the brutality of their policy of ethnic cleansing and Aryan superiority became known, it is hard to grasp the sense of relief our family and our people felt.

My father's life was saved by the arrival of the Germans. My mother was still in hiding. As a child of nine years old, I knew nothing of the persecution of Jewish men, women and children by the Nazi SS. I knew nothing of the concentration camps. I only knew my fear of losing first one parent, then the other. Already, my father's brother had disappeared. My mother's brothers were somewhere, dead perhaps, perhaps in the Soviet army, or exiled to the east. With the Germans came hope that perhaps what had already been done to us could somehow be undone, that Artur and Karli would return. And, for me, I still had no way of knowing if my mother had been sent east, if she was safe for the moment and if I might see her again. I only knew that my father was by some miracle of fate back home. The presence of the Germans had put almost everything back as it had been.

My father did not return to his school or his position as principal. Instead, he spent the years of German occupation working as a housing supervisor in a small town, Kohtla-Nõmme, where he, Elsa and Taavet moved after his release and recovery. The Germans didn't just take over the country. They directed the citizens of Estonia to assist them in their war against Russia. Despite what we viewed as liberation from the Soviets, our lives were not without fear. A single false move, a phrase or indication of a state of mind disloyal to the current occupiers could result in severe consequences. Of course, I knew nothing of this as a child. I learned it all much later. Like anyone's routine from day to day, on the surface of life, there were some joys to remember and cherish.

PART II

Narva

Narva River with the two cidadels; Estonia on the
left, Russia on the right.

CHAPTER 7

Mother returned to me but not before the summer was nearly over. Amanda, my mother's dear friend, hid her and kept her safe. All I knew is that Amanda lived near the seashore in the town of Sillamäe where Mother and I had once lived, and that my mother did not leave Amanda's apartment for the duration of her disappearance. She managed to send a note to my father to tell of her whereabouts, and later to my Grandmother Olga but by then I was out of communication and living in the bunker by the river. Soon after the Germans arrived my father took me back to the farm in Mahu and the welcoming arms of Grandmother Olga. I stayed there waiting for Mother to return. It took a bit longer than I expected and despite Grandmother's assurances that she was safe, I worried silently until I saw her.

I wasn't sitting on the porch facing the road when she arrived. I wasn't actively thinking about her; I was milking a cow with Uncle Julius when I heard her voice. All I heard was a single syllable of a word. I can't remember what it was she was saying. I just felt it, there, mingled with Aunt Ellen's voice, and there she was. I was through the barn and halfway to the house and there she stood, arms open, stooped over, waiting to lift me for a hug. And all was as it should be. I remember thinking that, feeling that. This is the way things are supposed to be. And that was that.

Mother quietly answered my questions but with very little to tell since she'd spent all her time inside, in hiding, and was cut off from just about everything except what Amanda could tell her. I told her far more, and Toivo laughed at me as Mother tried to take in all the stories of the summer, of Father's arrest, of the bunker and the arrival of the Germans. But Mother listened to every last word. By the end of that first evening, Toivo stopped laughing at me, particularly after I told the story about my rescue of Taavet when they came for my father.

It was autumn and time for school for both of us, so Mother and I moved to Narva, where Uncle Leonhard helped her find a job. Narva is the easternmost city in

Mother (on right) with
best friend Amanda

Estonia, just across the Narva River from Leningrad, Russia. My memory of my first impression of Narva is that it is very old. Its streets, prior to their destruction during this war, were cobblestone, and the buildings were of stone or wood, precisely constructed and quite beautifully designed. Third Elementary School became my school and my mother's place of work. My Uncle Artur had taught music at this same school. Artur's reputation and Leonhard's position as a well-known lawyer in Narva surely helped my mother obtain her teaching position. While we lived there during the German occupation my Uncle Leonhard was appointed mayor. Our home in Narva was a single story house with a walled garden. The owners, we learned, had been sent by the Soviets to Siberia. It was odd to live in such a house. I imagined a knock on the door one day, a strange family standing on the step, feeling strangely self-conscious as they knocked on the front door of their own home instead of unlocking it and walking in as they were entitled. I imagined opening the door and inviting them inside. What would happen next? Would I invite them for dinner and share our rationed food with them? Complete strangers? Probably. We shared whatever we had, no matter how scarce, and in Narva during this time, when fresh food was hard to find my mother and I were lucky. Grandmother Olga and my aunts and uncles sent food to us from the farm -- meats and fresh vegetables. Of course we'd share. Then, what? Would my mother, Amanda and I move out and give them back their home?

Uncle Leonhard

Would they stay here with us? We had a side room, an extra empty room. They could stay there. Sometimes, we'd rent out that little space to make a little extra money. What about the furnishings and the linens and all their possessions that we used every day? And the gooseberry jam we canned in the summer? Those gooseberry bushes in the yard, I counted them one day, 142 bushes. Mother and I picked so many it was impossible to eat them all. So we made jam and enjoyed them far into the winter. There must have been hundreds of jars in the basement keeping cool. Who would keep those? But, the owners of our house never returned; most of those sent east never did.

Grandmother Olga did not spend the winters with us in Narva. This was wartime. German soldiers were everywhere in this easternmost of Estonian cities, a major supply depot for the battle raging in Leningrad. The train station was heavily guarded by the German army. Most of the food produced in Estonia was commandeered for the soldiers. Our civilian food was rationed. Ration coupons were issued in sheets each month. They stated how many grams of sugar, milk and bread we could purchase, if these items happened to be available at any of the local stores. Each day, after school, it was my job to hunt up food for the three of us. How well I did at the markets determined how well we ate. Most often, I would walk home from school with my friend, Aino Niine, but while I did I kept a close eye on each of the food stores we passed. On any given day, I would pass by and see a line forming. That would be a signal that the store had received a shipment of something important. I'd go up to the line and ask what they were waiting to buy. "Sugar," might be the answer at one store. Or, it might be coffee, or bread, or milk. I'd run home and leave my school things and grab our ration coupons and return to the store and get in line. It might take hours to obtain a small bit of sugar. Then I'd make the rounds to the other stores and see what they had received. I'd get in another line and so it would continue until I'd be out of time or until the stores closed up shop for the day or ran out of goods. The Germans needed food for their army. So much of the food produced in my country was taken away to feed the soldiers there was little left for the people. We subsisted on a very basic diet, mostly cabbage and potatoes. But, because of the family farm we were able to get a wider variety of foods than most of our neighbors, extra flour, smoked meats, barley and potatoes.

Why Narva, I ask now? Why would my mother choose to live in this occupied city? Yes, Uncle Leonhard and his wife, Maanja were here. The Germans certainly kept the Soviets away from us. But soon, when the bombing started, we no longer felt safe.

Attending school again was a welcome return to normalcy, although, like every end of summer it was hard to leave my cousins and the place that was the heart of our family. This year was particularly hard because so much had happened. We still knew nothing of Uncle Artur or Uncle Karli. Despite the German soldiers everywhere along the roads between Mahu and Narva, we did not feel fear. Yes, it was nothing like other summers when our country was free, but, compared to what we knew of Soviet crimes

With best friend Aino

against our people, the German's seemed like liberators.

Mother was pleased to be busy teaching. I walked to school past a park, Pimeaed. Aino and I crossed a wide, open square where soldiers would guide us past traffic and greet us with polite smiles. Most days, it was quiet, somber, walking through the occupied city of Narva with German soldiers stationed everywhere. We were polite in return. When the Germans knew a battle might be coming they systematically evacuated civilians before any fighting began. Later this was to play an important role in our fate, but there is more to tell of Narva first.

Life wasn't all fear and war and worry. There is always time for play and I managed, with my friend Aino, to find time to study, to play, and to enjoy life. The house we rented was at Raja 16, and it stood seven houses away from the rails where the trains brought supplies and German soldiers to Narva. The city had taken over both the house and the responsibility of renting it out. The government did that with every empty house, probably with the intent of keeping it from squatters or from vandals, in the event the rightful owners ever returned. That, of course, didn't happen, at least not in Narva, because by the end of the war ninety-five percent of the city was destroyed by Soviet bombs. I remember the house quite clearly though. It was a single story and I can visualize the layout of the rooms, a living room, a small dining room, the kitchen, bedrooms, and a small extra room where we might allow someone to stay for a small amount of rent. And the yard! How someone managed to have such a big yard in the middle of the city was a mystery to us. But I mentioned the 142 gooseberry bushes already. I didn't mention the apple and cherry trees and the colors of the fruit as they ripened -- red, yellow, green and such a treat. We didn't take fresh fruit for granted in Narva. The yard was one of my favorite places. Aino and I played there. I loved that special place, all except the view from the backyard of a huge red Russian church that taunted us, and reminded us of fear and of those who disappeared on the trains. Perhaps the view of that church reminded us to be grateful for the German's success in driving the Russians out of Estonia. I was certainly grateful to have my mother back and my father alive.

I returned to Narva, once, as an adult, with my husband and children. That was in the year 1978. We had flown into Tallinn and were only allowed by the Soviet government to stay at a hotel, not with Uncle Artur and his wife in their house in Tallinn-Nomme, the suburb of the capital city. Uncle Artur did not want to visit us in our hotel room during that trip. He wanted to see us anywhere in Tallinn but in that room. Not that it was a bad room; it was quite comfortable even by Soviet standards. What made Artur nervous? I noticed Artur whispering in his conversations all the while we were in that hotel. "Why are you whispering?" I asked.

He leaned close and said in my ear, "They plant microphones and they listen to every word we say."

"Why?" I asked. "We are just visiting our family."

Artur said. "You are Estonian exiles. So you are considered possible spies."

Arvid, my husband, heard that and laughed. Artur did not. He just went pale and uncomfortable with his eyes darting toward corners and light fixtures and the underside of tables. And suddenly, Arvid was speaking very, very loudly and voicing some very strong views of the Soviet occupiers. My ears perked up. Arvid was behaving like an American citizen. That's because he was an American citizen, and he was protected under our constitution's Bill of Rights. We are guaranteed freedom of expression. Soviet citizens have been known to disappear forever because of the things they say. And, Arvid was saying things to frighten Artur.

"Arvid," I said. "Shhh."

He only talked the louder. He criticized the airport, the streetlights, the scarcity of basic goods people needed to live, all the things we had noticed since our arrival. He went on quite a long time. All the while, Artur, who held an important teaching professorship at the Music Conservatory of Tallinn, sweated and frowned.

Arvid did not realize that Artur could suffer the consequences of his political commentary. He and I and our children could just get on an airplane and fly to our home and our freedom, but Artur, if anyone from the secret police heard him, could lose everything, including his life. I began to scan the hotel room for hidden microphones. I wasn't sure if I wanted to silence Arvid or reassure Uncle Artur. Under the sofa, high inside the curtains on the windows, under the beds, I searched. And sure enough, I found several. To drive Artur even further with worry, Arvid brought his face close to the one by the curtains, "What do you think of that, KGB?"

I learned on that trip that the Soviet government was so afraid of groups who might try to overthrow the government center in Moscow that they printed and sold maps that led people to roads that didn't exist. This was part of their national security! We were just a family of four in the country to see our relatives.

We wanted to visit Narva. More accurately, I wanted to visit Narva. Arvid hadn't been there, but it was important to me because I'd spent so much time there as a child, so I applied for a permit to drive there from Tallinn. On the first day I was turned down. On the second day when I made my application I was turned down again. Same on the third and fourth and finally, on the fifth day the officer at the ministry agreed under the condition that we return to Tallinn and report in to them before dark on the day we traveled. It was a fight, but I won and I thought back to other times when I had to go up against someone in a uniform and I'd prevailed. But I'll tell those stories later. We were going to Narva!

Getting back by dark would not be a problem. Estonia is so far north the days are long in summer. Daylight lingers well past eleven o'clock. So we set out in Uncle Artur's car on the one road that leads from Tallinn east to Narva. I remember that road well, although now, thirty-four years after I fled my country, it looked much different. The Soviets had erected watchtowers and little booths along the road. These booths were checkpoints. Uncle Artur, I noticed, was very nervous as we set out. He drove. Arvid sat in the front passenger seat and I climbed in the rear with my children, Reino, 13, and Sirike, 17. It wasn't long before Arvid was the nervous one. Artur drove at precisely the speed limit, which was forty kilometers per hour. The drive was two hundred kilometers, which, at Artur's rate of speed would take five hours.

"Pull over," Arvid requested, his politeness strained.

"We can't," Artur said. "Not until we get to the first check point."

"If you don't pull over, we will never get to the first check point," Arvid said.

The security apparatus knew what time we had left Tallinn. We'd been informed when I obtained the papers that if we did not arrive at the first checkpoint within a reasonable time for the distance, there would be a warrant issued for our arrest. Quite possibly the security police would begin to search for us. Artur, on one hand, was afraid of arrest for driving over the very strict speed limit. But Arvid was also right. At Artur's speed we'd arrive in Narva with just enough time to turn around and return to Tallinn.

"I'll drive," Arvid said. "We'll get to the check point just fine."

Artur, relieved of the responsibility of obeying the law, pulled over. Arvid got out and took Artur's place behind the wheel. We took off at a fast pace and the countryside now slid past us at a good clip. Artur, now in the passenger seat, said nothing and from the back seat I could not see his face. Arvid told me later Artur frowned through the whole drive and his face was bright red. Eventually, we approached the first checkpoint and a policeman gestured for Arvid to roll down the window. Artur turned around. "Just sit tight," he said to my son Reino. "Try to smile."

Arvid, I could tell, found the very idea of a checkpoint offensive and I silently prayed he would resist the urge to challenge the guard. To my relief, and I'm sure Artur's as well, Arvid behaved himself and complied with the guard's request for identification papers. "American tourists," Arvid said and I detected a challenge in his voice. It was quite unusual for foreigners to travel independently from city to city. The uniformed guard bent over and sent a sharp glance into the back seat where my children and I offered innocent smiles. He was a young man, very tall with curly hair that stuck out from under his cap. Any feelings of fear and worry that had come over me as we approached dissipated. He was barely older than my daughter! He went to his booth for a moment or two and returned. "Where were you?" he asked.

"What do you mean? We were in Tallinn." Arvid responded with a tinge of annoyance. He turned to Artur. "See, we drove too slow."

"Where did you stop?" the guard asked again.

"We stopped to change seats," Arvid said. "It's your speed limit."

The guard peered over the edge of our papers and scrutinized my husband. "Why did you change seats? Stopping is not allowed. Where did you stop?"

"Along the road. We pulled over and I got in here, Artur moved over. May we continue our trip please?"

"You may not stop," the guard said.

"What if I have to go to the bathroom?" I could now see that Arvid was beginning to have some fun with this guard.

"You must wait until you arrive," said the guard firmly.

"But you know, what if I can't? I've got kids with me."

"What are their ages?" he studied our papers again. "Who is who?" he asked, studying our passports.

"I am Imbi, their mother," I said. "This is my daughter Sirike and my son Reino. Is there a bathroom here we can use?"

"Not allowed," he replied.

"Then you must allow us extra time, just in case," Arvid said. "I have a problem you know. I was in the war and..." In the back seat, I started to laugh. Arvid was in the US military but he didn't suffer any injury. He was playing with this man, trying to make him squirm, seeing how far he would go to enforce the rules. "Is it against the rules to water the grass?" Arvid started to open his door to get out.

"Sir, you are not allowed to um, to, uh, to use the..."

Arvid just started to laugh and shut his door with a gentle thud. "Okay. I'll hold it until I get to Narva."

The guard looked relieved. He turned his attention to the back seat, sticking his head through the window to study Sirike and Reino and their passport photos. The kids were laughing at their father's bathroom humor.

Our guard stiffened and pulled his head back and nearly bumped the window with his cap. Arvid said, "Watch it there."

Artur just sat and stared straight ahead. In a few seconds, the policeman handed back our papers and Arvid jerked the car forward and off we were.

"That was easier than I expected," Arvid said, his foot pressing the accelerator. I saw him glance at Artur. "What's wrong?"

Artur said, "Nothing, Arvid. They will use any excuse to make us turn back."

"Can't these people take a joke?"

"No.

"Arvid," I said on Artur's behalf, "please just do only what they ask. Poor Artur. If we stir up trouble, it'll be his trouble. We can just call the American embassy and they'll protect us. Artur has no protection. We don't want them to send him to Siberia."

"Not again, thank you," Artur said. "I spent enough years there."

In 1941, when my mother disappeared into hiding with her friend Amanda, Artur had fled Narva and found his way to Tallinn hoping, as many young people hoped in those days, to get on a ship and head west to escape the Soviet invasion of our country. I can only imagine that Leonhard, who lived in Narva at that time, urged him to do this. "You are of recruitment age," I can hear Uncle Leonhard telling him. "You'll become a Soviet soldier or, if you refuse, they'll send you into exile or shoot you." So, how Artur made his way to Tallinn is as much a mystery to me as how my mother made her way to Amanda's. But, he made it to Tallinn only to find the Soviets mobilizing all the young men. Artur boarded an east-bound ship that brought him and countless other young men to Leningrad, Russia against their will. Here they were forced to sign up and join the Soviet army, or meet another fate. But little did he know that his brother Karli was facing the same set of circumstances.

Karli too had been in Tallinn. He had dreamed, growing up as the son of a blacksmith, that he would one day sail the world and so, as a young man he found his way to Tallinn and a job as a mate for a commercial shipping company. He too, when the Soviets arrived, was loaded onto an east-bound ship and arrived in Leningrad around the same time as Artur.

With astonishment, one evening, while walking along in the port, these two brothers chanced to meet. Imagine the thrill they felt seeing each other there! At that time there was severe famine in Leningrad. Karli, a handsome six-footer and athletic young man appeared to his brother like a skeleton. He weighed less than one hundred pounds and described that out of desperate hunger they were eating rats, soap and anything on board their ship. Tree roots, if found, were a delicacy. They embraced and spent a few hours exchanging stories. Neither knew what the future held, but they promised to carry the news of each other, if they could, back to the family in Estonia. How that would be accomplished was anyone's guess. The two young men parted and the family didn't learn of the fate of either until the end of the war.

Artur returned to his floating barracks and soon afterwards an officer gathered the men and asked them, "Does any one of you know anything about music?"

Artur, not knowing why such a question was asked, raised his hand. "I am a music teacher. I trained at the conservatory in Tallinn."

Nobody else raised his hand. "Come with me," said the officer.

Russians, as a nation, appreciate music very deeply. Artur was taken east to a labor camp. His job, for the next several years, was to conduct an orchestra that played symphonies to boost morale while the Soviet soldiers dug mass graves -- long shallow trenches -- and buried the dead. These camps were cold, desolate and the prisoners had little shelter or food. Their only clothing was whatever they'd worn on their backs as they were loaded onto the trains and transported there. Many died of exposure in the harsh Siberian winter. Disease was common and if men became too weak to work they were shot to death.

While Arvid drove us to Narva, Artur told this story to my children. In 1978, thirty-four years later, the fear of being sent into exile for disobedience of Soviet law was as real to Uncle Artur as it was in 1941. He was one of the lucky ones. He had musical talent the Soviets had found use for. Later, as the war progressed and the eastern front of the war with Germany grew bitter and fierce, Artur was shipped to the fighting front where again he led the army band to the beat of marches while the Soviets buried their dead. These dead were not the exiled prisoners of the labor camps. These were dead soldiers who lost their lives fighting the war. He witnessed the burial of thousands of soldiers into common graves, never to be found by their families.

Uncle Artur

Uncle Artur never escaped from the oppressive presence of the Soviets. He did escape death in the harsh places he was sent and was forever aware of how very close he came to sharing the fate of many of his fellow Estonian citizens. When the Soviets re-took Estonia in 1944 Uncle Artur came back to his country with them. He, in 1978, was a professor of music at the conservatory in Tallinn, and conductor of the Estonian Male Chorus for ten years, traveling and bringing music to the countries behind the Iron Curtain. Newly composed Estonian songs praising Stalin and Russian music were performed. Estonian traditional music was forbidden.

We had ulterior motives on that road-trip to Narva. My request for permission to leave the city of Tallinn did not tell the Soviet authorities of this other desire in my heart. Grandmother Olga has died in 1962. My heart longed to visit her grave and say a prayer and pay her my respects. I knew, after the first few rejections of my request to drive to Narva, that the authorities would never give us permission to take a side trip to Viru-Nigula, and the cemetery, which was only a half kilometer east off the main road. But, I would not go home to New Jersey before I fulfilled this wish.

The checkpoint guards were correct when they asked us if we stopped along the way. We had. But we kept silent at their question. I had instructed my children to smile and say nothing and to leave any of the soldier's questions to Arvid and me.

Our relatives knew of our arrival in Tallinn. They also knew that the area of the coastline where our farm had been was off limits to anyone but the residents of that locale. As United States citizens we were foreigners and we could not visit or even drive through that part of Estonia. Under most circumstances we would not even have been allowed to leave Tallinn. We were not allowed to go to Uncle

Artur's home or stay anywhere but at the Viru Hotel. But, word had traveled to our loved ones in Estonia that we would be there, so together we selected a point about halfway along the road to Narva and designated it as our family reunion spot.

There we were, at just about the same place along that road where my German general turned off toward Mahu[1], Arvid pulled the car over where our friends and relatives had arrived, on foot, in cars, on bicycles, to visit us the only way they could. Here we were, on the main road having a huge family reunion. It was here that we brought out the many gifts we had brought from home. My children helped me open bags and take out American blue jeans, sneakers, sweaters -- all sorts of things we had expertly hidden in our luggage. We knew what was allowed in and what was not. I had packed our ten suitcases very carefully with our clothing on the top and bottom and sides of each suitcase, but the inner layer of each bag was the hiding place for all these forbidden goods.

The rules allowed us to bring in some clothing but no yard fabric, so my mother, the expert seamstress, had spent weeks selecting fabric at stores back home in the US and sewing a few seams into them so they resembled dresses and skirts. But once in Estonia we pulled these rows of stitches out and smoothed the fabric flat again so our relatives, who had no access to stores or goods we took so for granted in the US, could make clothes for themselves. Of course, everyone was delighted to see us, with or without our smuggled gifts, and we spent a good hour or so sharing news and taking pictures and giving hugs and kisses all around.

Renate, my dear cousin, and I had corresponded occasionally for years. I knew she had married and had children. I also knew of those who had passed away. It is the custom in Estonia, when visiting, to bring flowers, so there at the roadside bouquet after bouquet was handed around among us. Renate's husband Leo said to me, "Imbi, shall I take you to visit Olga?"

It was forbidden. The graveyard was very close to the main road. Between it and us were mainly a few trees, but we knew this was a forbidden trip. Renate and he knew how much it would mean for me to go there. It is also an Estonian custom to keep our graves in well-tended condition, with flowers laid at the head stones, weeds and debris cleaned away and visits for prayers on special holidays of remembrance. It meant a lot to me that he offered to take me there. So, in a few minutes we had a plan. He would drive me to the graveyard, alone, so as to not draw attention to ourselves. Everyone else, the rest of the family, would remain here until my return.

So off we went. As we drove off, I saw the concerned look on the faces of my children who already knew of the hidden microphones in our hotel room and for whom the story of Uncle Artur's exile and fear was so very fresh. I remembered

---

[1] This story is told in Chapter 8.

my own mother, long ago on that morning in June, 1941, heading off alone to the forest. This fed my resolve to overcome any obstacles in returning to them.

There we were, Leo and I, arriving at the graveyard close to a small church, Leo guiding me to Grandmother Olga's grave, recognizing my grandfather's grave I'd not seen for decades but which I visited at times with Mother, and walking solemnly through the well cared for stones of other families. I imagined a soldier in Soviet drab colors appearing and falling into step directly behind us. I shivered from fear all the while I paid my respects to my grandmother and placed one of the small bouquets of flowers gently upon her grave. When I stepped back to bow my head to pray, Leo stepped back too. Religion is not recognized in the Soviet republics. I imagined being arrested simply for praying in a somewhat public place, so I did not say any prayer out loud, but simply stood with my head bowed and my hands dangling at my sides instead of joined together. Leo did the same. It was maddening to know we could be scrutinized and invaded in this private moment. I was so sure that had Arvid come with me he would not be able to endure the intimidation I felt just imagining what could happen, and that all three of us could have ended up in the gulag if anyone had seen us. The fear of the possibilities kept me silent and secretive in this very small but important moment of my visit.

We didn't stay long. We walked stiffly back to Leo's car and drove off. I didn't dare look back. We used the rearview mirror to check to see if we were followed.

Back with the family, my fear did not leave immediately. The sight of everyone together was a reminder that even this small gathering of family was seen as an illegal meeting and could draw trouble. I just wanted to disperse and get back in the car to Narva. My children hugged me tight as I emerged from the car.

"You were gone so long," said Reino. "What took so long?"

"The drive is longer than I remembered," I said. I'd been gone just barely an hour. My mother had been gone for three months. My children knew far more of the potential dangers to me than I knew at age nine so I knew why an hour could seem to go on forever. We eventually kissed and hugged everyone, bid them good-bye and turned the car toward the east to Narva.

After several more checkpoints and with a bit of somber new understanding of Uncle Artur's fear, as well as some of our own, we pulled into Narva, or, should I say, what was left of the Narva of my youthful days. During World War II it was mostly destroyed. What was destroyed during the battle of Narva was replaced with gray, depressing, poorly constructed buildings the Soviets erected rapidly to provide housing and to encourage Russians to cross the border and settle in Estonian territory. It was not the city of my youth any longer, but I was determined to find something -- anything familiar to show my children. The streets themselves were different, running in different directions, named in the

Russian language, with no landmarks to prompt memory of places I knew so well as a child.

We attempted to find somewhere to eat lunch but the only restaurant we could find told us they had no food to serve. We were quite hungry after our long car drive and had brought no food with us. The employees at the restaurant said they had no food to serve us and there were no other restaurants to be found. "But, go upstairs," said a woman. "Maybe we can find some soup for you."

The five of us climbed the stairs and sat quietly down at a small table. A woman in drab gray clothing with a headscarf brought us five bowls of soup and some dark Russian bread. It was a thin clear soup with not much in it, but the bread was crusty and delicious. We ate gratefully. They spoke only a small bit of our language. It struck us that Narva had been taken over by Russian-speaking people. Our culture and our language had suffered from the influx of Russian speaking natives who crossed the border to Estonia, sent by Stalin to work in the shale oil plant just west of the city. Narva showed us the impact the Sovietization of our society had done. Collectivization and communism had destroyed the infrastructure of the capitalist society we had left so long ago. Nobody owned anything. Only the state was allowed to own property or to hire workers. The restaurant did not belong to the kind people who fed us. It belonged to the state. If no food was provided, nobody lost any income from the lack of food. They most likely were hoarding the food for their own consumption, a hedge against starvation, but they were kind enough to share with us, guests in their country.

Once we had our bit of nourishment, we were back outside and on the streets of my familiar city, but there was so little that had survived it was almost impossible for me to show my children anything at all from my childhood. The city hall was still standing, but ninety-five percent of the city had been destroyed by bombs during the three year German occupation and the final battle of Narva. January 1944 was the last time I had seen Narva. As I walked, I took in the cheap structures and the poorly maintained streets and remembered what had been, cobblestone avenues, majestic buildings, but all I could do was describe for my children what had once been here. There was the city hall. I knew that city hall so well when Uncle Leonhard had been mayor. It was strong, and the basement was dug well down into the earth under its thick, stone walls. Its vaulted cellar was our refuge on the clear nights when the planes came. The bomber pilots needed the moonlight and stars to guide them across the landscape and to find their targets. For three years, they came just about every clear night. I wished in my mind that I could paint the moon black. I mentioned earlier that our house was only seven houses away from the rail line where the supply trains to the eastern front were lined up. That was the target for the Soviet planes. Night after night, they came. The drone as they came in, the whistling of the bombs, followed by popping and roaring of explosions. Some small, some, if they hit the ammunition depots on the German lines, huge firestorms of sound and flame.

Amanda, Mother's friend, worked at the city clerk's office at that time. And, Uncle Leonhard, of course, was there in daylight almost daily. But, Mother and I spent our nights there, down in that deep stone fortress of a basement, with marble steps and heavy carved stone walls, safe, or so we prayed, safe from the fire and the destruction, everything but the sounds that seemed to go on and on and on, until finally, when the sun rose and day came, the droning of the planes would cease, the sound of bombs and their loud insistent thunder would be replaced by the morning birds singing their happy songs. I sat, with my mother and Amanda, sometimes with Uncle Leonhard and his wife Maanja on the small stone ledge that ran along the tunneling hallway of that basement refuge, sitting, maybe lying with my head on a pillow if I'd managed to grab one from home as we made our hurried way to this shelter. Other people from our lives came for shelter too. Often the long corridor was crowded with families; I counted three hundred people sitting with us one long night. We would sit in silence, praying they would not drop any directly overhead. Sleep, of course, was impossible. By

seven in the morning, after being awake all night, we would find our way out of the vaulted cellar and head home. New waves of destruction greeted us, smoldering ruins where homes once stood, and I would get home, dress and head to school walking past demolished houses, wondering if the inhabitants were alive. Often, I'd walk past stunned families, who returned home as I did to find a pile of rubble where their home had been. There would be tears mingled with cries of relief that they weren't home when the bomb hit.

Seven houses from the rail line, our home was still intact in January 1944 when the Germans evacuated Narva of all civilians. I returned from city hall each morning to behold my house had survived yet another night of the onslaught. Mother

Narva City Hall

and Amanda and I often stood feeling a sense of relief, but on one particular morning that feeling was short-lived. The neighborhood had been hit. We walked slowly around to our huge back yard to check the fruit trees and the garden. From there we could see our next-door neighbor's house had been utterly destroyed. I walked around the garden, noticing the 142 gooseberry bushes were still standing, totally intact and with buds still promising fruit. But I stopped short as I took this in. For there, under the gooseberry bushes was a sight no child, no human being should ever be required to see. There, on the ground, under my precious gooseberry bushes, was the head, only the head, of our next-door neighbor. Mother saw it as I did, at the same time, with the same horror. She pulled me away and hid my eyes. "Imbi," she said. "Don't look. Go inside, please."

But I didn't move. I stood, trembling at the sight. I took in the hushed, raging sense of despair and disgust and sorrow that welled up in my chest, while my pulse pounded in my ears, and panic filled my every vein and cell and nerve ending. I looked up. There, gleaming with a sneering grimace, was the steeple of the massive Russian church, looming over the wall from just beyond our back yard, strong, always stark against the sky. That church had always been there, always reminding us of the Russian border not that very far away, a symbol of the menacing enemy who threatened our very lives. After that day, each glimpse of that church brought back that moment of terrible anguish and fear and sorrow. I still helped Mother pick gooseberries to prepare our jars for winter but I averted my eyes from the ground underneath all those richly laden bushes. And from that church with its bulb-like steeple I turned my face so I would not be tempted to pray for its destruction and for the destruction of our enemies.

The railway was eventually destroyed by Soviet bombs. But when I started school in Narva I saw the railroad tracks on my way to and from Elementary Three every day. This was my tenth year on this earth and I enjoyed school. I worked hard but Aino and I had fun too. I remember most our afternoons, once I'd managed the ration lines, when we spent hours with dolls fashioned out of paper and cardboard. We fashioned clothes for the dolls, also out of paper. Today the stores sell sets of paper dolls with colorful clothing already drawn and printed on sheets of paper -- pages and pages of dresses, coats, pants, accessories and hats. Back then we designed and cut out our own designs from paper and sometimes from scraps of fabric. My mother, the woman who had created beautiful clothing for herself, admired the meticulous attention to detail in my doll clothes designs. I shared them with Aino and she shared hers with me. We spent many hours in this pursuit. And, often we'd run home after school to resume a game with our paper dolls, a game we might have spent many hours at school dreaming up.

Soldiers everywhere. Narva was an occupied city. Aino and I walked and skipped home from school and I suppose it was much easier for us to ignore the soldiers than it was for the adults. We felt safe. They'd keep the Russians out of

Estonia. The broken cross – the swastika -- the symbol for the German National Socialist Party, the Nazi's, was a familiar symbol. The men wore it. Pictures of German rulers showed them in front of banners and flags displaying this symmetrical, geometrical emblem of their strength. At that time we did not know about the horrors of the death camps. Our fear lay in the night and in the anticipation of Soviet planes flying and dropping their bombs on our city as we slept.

The siege of Leningrad, today returned to its original name, St. Petersburg, began in September 1941, about the time my mother and I moved to Narva. These two cities were very close to each other. As a matter of fact, Narva was so close to the fighting that the German's took over several school buildings and used them as hospital facilities for the wounded soldiers transported from the front lines. Elementary Three was one of those schools, so my class moved and shared a building some distance away. Elementary Three used the classrooms of the higher school from seven until noon and another principal and staff took over in the afternoons for a whole new collection of students. Aino and I had a longer walk home but we had long afternoons for other things, after I made my rationing rounds of the stores, of course.

One clear afternoon Aino and I walked home as usual. We arrived at the center of Narva, a wide plaza busy with civilians coming and going under the watchful eye of the occupying Germans. First we heard a soft murmur approaching from the east. Then the sound grew louder until it dawned on us. That familiar drone was only heard at night, and only on cloudless, clear nights when the moon shed its light on the city and all its surroundings. These were nights when the Russians dropped their bombs on the German trains and anything else in the vicinity. As I recognized that sound, so did everyone else in that plaza. Everyone ran for cover! Then we looked up and the planes swooped in low. But they were German planes, the broken cross of the German swastika clearly etched into the underside of each aircraft. The confusion was clear on our faces and in our hesitation. Then, the planes, just above rooftops, opened a rat-tat-tat-tat of gunfire on the open plaza and the first victims dropped to the ground. Another wave of planes and that sound again. Not bombs but machine-gun fire. These planes aimed at people, not freight cars! Aino and I broke into a run. Everyone ran. The soldiers shouted, "Stop! Don't run!"

Nobody listened. These were German planes trying to kill us and the German occupiers were telling us to stop? Aino and I fled for our lives. We were in a mad dash when suddenly someone grabbed me by my ankle and I was flat on my stomach on the ground and so was Aino. "Stay down!" A German soldier lay on the ground next to us. "Play dead!" he said. "Don't move a muscle!"

We obeyed. I could see citizens falling to the ground. Some were tripped by the soldiers and went flying down. Others were hit by gunfire and died right there in front of us. The planes came and came, waves of them, and yes, I wanted to get up and run to safety, but I saw how right our soldier, lying there next to us on the pavement was. I didn't move. I barely breathed. I could see Aino. She was on the ground too. I wanted to move my head. Was she alive or was she hit by a bullet? She was so still. I couldn't see if she was breathing or not. Surely, as I felt my own panicked breathing move my chest up and down, surely I could tell if she was breathing or not. But I couldn't. It seemed endless, but later we knew it was only a few short minutes and they were gone. The roar faded into the distant sky. Slowly, a soldier lifted his head. "All clear!" he announced. And people began to move. Aino lifted her head. "Imbi!" she said. Our soldier sat up. I pushed myself to a sit and stared at him. "You tripped me."

"Yes, and it saved your life."

"They were German planes," I said.

"No," he answered. "They were Soviet planes. I know my planes. They were Soviet made."

"But..." I was about to say the German symbol was clear as day on them.

"They must have painted it on to get past our defense," he said, so assuredly that I believed him immediately. "Don't trust what you see."

But should I trust him? Why would he know this? He just saved my and Aino's lives. That was why. We stood up. Others were getting up and moving out of the square. Many others did not get up and never would. The soldiers went to work caring for the wounded and carrying away the dead. Aino and I fled the clearing, walking rapidly away, holding hands, glancing up toward the sky, knowing that just because it was clear now didn't mean it would stay so. Home was our destination. No food stores for me today. Mother kept me inside and walked Aino to her home. That was one of the few times planes came to Narva in the daytime. But, on the nights when the sky was crystal clear and stars glimmered alongside the moon, the planes always came. For three long years, they came until I began to wish I could paint the moon black and extinguish its light. I prayed daily for rain and cloud cover so we could get a good night's rest.

My family, or I should say, my mother's family, was a musical family. Not only Uncle Artur could be counted among the musically talented. Aunt Ellen, in Mahu, sang her way through her busy days. At night, someone always played an accordion, a guitar or sang. Estonia is a place filled with music and despite the hardship, or perhaps because of the hardship, music was an important part of all of our lives. In Narva, during those years of the German occupation, I took piano lessons and I was expected to practice every day. But, in our small rented house with the huge back yard, there was no piano. To practice, I had to visit Uncle Leonhard's huge fancy house one block from the central square.

Uncle Leonhard's home was quite beautiful. He encouraged me to play. I walked to his house with my music sheets and sat at his grand piano in a beautiful room to pound out my lessons. I was not very good and I did not enjoy the practice sessions or having to walk that long distance through rain and snow.

In 1978, in Narva again after so many years, as we walked the unrecognizable streets, I told my children of my uncle's house and of the importance of music in our lives. I told them of the song festival Estonia had held every five years since 1869. Even during the Soviet occupation of fifty years, which lasted until 1991, the Song Festivals were held, but only songs to praise Stalin were allowed.

I did not tell my children of the frightening nights of bombing, of that afternoon scare in the square or of my neighbor's severed head among the gooseberry bushes.

I was determined to find the house where I'd lived but everything was so confusing. Even the rail lines were not where they once had been, the cheap buildings and new town layout simply added to the sense of strangeness. Most of the citizens of Narva in 1978 did not speak Estonian, only Russian. Finally, I noticed a group of men standing on a street corner. I approached them and asked, in Estonian, "Do you know where 16 Raja Street is?" Two out of three did not understand me. The third, however, spoke Estonian. "I know where Raja Street was," he said, "come with me."

My family must have looked strange to the people of Narva as we followed this kind stranger. Our American clothes and shoes signaled that we were visitors. My children were better dressed with American blue jeans and Nike sneakers. Even our hairstyles had a quality we take for granted in the United States. While we followed this man, I saw his shoes were worn out at the heels, his cuffs of his jacket were threadbare and his shirt underneath was missing a few buttons. His teeth were brown and one in the front was missing. Arvid seemed so robust walking alongside him, questioning him about his background, his family, his remembrance of the past. Perhaps he too was a child in Narva in 1941. He seemed older than me, but I reminded myself that life was hard and not very happy in this country. He led us through some twists and turns, right, left, then right again, when suddenly he stopped. "Here," he said, "is the spot your house once stood."

I looked. And, there, right under our feet, was a little patch of green grass surrounded by rubble. This area had not been rebuilt. Or, if it had, it had been demolished again. I felt it more than I saw it, but I knew we were on Raja Street, this one patch of green in the middle of the city of Narva was where our house had been. I stood and remembered. I looked up and there, just to the west, was the tall tower of the Russian church. Right there, minus the cherry tree, minus the peach tree and the apple tree and, I looked around, minus the gooseberry bushes, here was the back yard of my childhood home.

"Here we are!" I cried. "My house was right here." My children looked doubtful. "See that church? I prayed that church would fall. Every day I hoped their own bombs would destroy their church." And, with an ache of remembrance

I would not share with my children, a tear escaped from my eye. That church still stood. But, memory flooded in from the days that followed that morning when I found my neighbor's head on the ground. That church was still standing, but more importantly, after all these years and after all the struggles, so was I. And so was Arvid. And, so was my mother.

CHAPTER 8

The bombing continued nightly. My days at school became less and less important as exhaustion set in for both my mother and me. It became nearly impossible to keep up with lessons and get to school after a night of huddling in the vaulted cellar of city hall. Finally my mother sent me to my father for rest, after she found me trembling in my bed, teeth chattering, tears flowing on a night we waited too long to make the decision to spend the night in the basement of city hall. Explosions, the scent of burning, sirens and flashes of firelight had shattered my fitful sleep. Mother took me into her bed and held me, soothing me, trying to calm my fear. I was ten years old. We had been living with nightly bombings and there was no end in sight. The battle of Leningrad raged on and on. The German supply depots were still in Narva. The next day, she packed a small bag for me, telegraphed my father and sent me to him. "To calm you," she said when she kissed me goodbye. "Don't worry, summer is coming and we'll go to Lauriveski."

Despite the battle waging in Leningrad, the roads in my country were safe for travel. It is unthinkable to imagine a young girl of ten or eleven traveling the highways alone in today's world, much less back then while a war was on, but that is exactly what I did. My mother walked with me to the main road, the same road I traveled in 1978 from Tallinn to Narva, and we waited for someone to come by in some sort of vehicle. Most Estonians of that period did not own cars, so when I stuck out my thumb to signal my need for a ride, often it was a German transport, a jeep or a wagon or a truck full of soldiers that would stop and let me get in. This first time, my mother lifted me up and a young soldier helped me settle onto a hard wooden seat alongside a line of young men carrying rifles and huge backpacks, wearing helmets and those vivid green German uniforms.

"How far can you take me?" I asked. I noticed a half smile cross my mother's face. A few hours ago I was trembling with fear in the night. Now, she saw a restored daughter, resolved again to a purpose, and I could see the relief on her face.

"How far would you like to go, Fraulein?"

"I am heading to Kohtla-Nomme to visit my father," I explained.

"Yes, we are going that way," said my young soldier. He looked at my mother. "She is safe here. Don't worry." And, despite a bit of uneasiness, I settled down onto my seat satisfied I would see my father in a few short hours. My mother blew me a kiss, spoke a bit to the soldier and waved as she let me go.

I would come to know this road well over the next few years. From 1941 to 1944 I traveled back and forth to my mother's and my father's homes, to

Lauriveski up north. The German soldiers were my unofficial chauffeurs, picking me up, dropping me at an intersection. There I would wait for a truck from a different direction to stop and let me in until I'd say, politely, "Thank-you, this is far enough." They'd let me out and I'd walk up the road to knock on the door of one of my many safe places to see family and friends. My new nickname was "the Gypsy" and I earned it well.

My memory of all these journeys is of kindness on the part of the drivers and the soldiers who must have enjoyed the company of a young girl who knew enough of their language to engage in conversation. Perhaps I reminded them of a sister or cousin or some child. Here they were, so far from home. And, who knew what they'd seen in this war. I look back and must say I always felt safe. There was never a worry about anyone hurting me. I'm sure if there had been any thought of that, my parents would never have let me travel this way. I relaxed and learned again how to sleep through the night at my father's house after that terrible case of nerves in Narva. Soon I was a child with very little responsibility. Elsa did the shopping, the rounds to the stores, the waiting in line for food. Often, I stayed at home to care for Taavet while she took care of those things, or I would accompany her, Taavet holding my hand while I distracted him from restlessness in his perambulator. I attended the local school while I stayed with my father. Soon it was summer and I knew it was again time to travel to the farm where I was sure Mother would return when school was finished.

I kissed my father and Elsa goodbye, patted Taavet on his fuzzy, curly head and with my small bag set off to find a ride north. I expected to travel west along the Tallinn/Narva road and walk the last seven kilometers north to Lauriveski from the terminus. My thumb was stuck out there for only a short while when a jeep screeched to a halt and I found myself face to face with a German general. I knew he was a general with his colorful braiding on his cap; his shoulders and chest were covered with medals and decorations signifying a high rank. He was in the back seat, another signal to me that he was an important man. A lieutenant stepped out of the back seat and saluted me. I returned the gesture with a bit of amusement. "Where are you headed, young lady?" he asked.

"Mahu," I answered.

"Where is your family?" he asked.

"They are in Mahu," I said.

He turned and spoke softly to the tall man with the decorations. In a few seconds he opened the door and stood back. "You may get in," he said formally.

"Thank-you," I said. He took my bag and held out a hand for me to take as I climbed into the back seat. Then he slammed the door. With a short bark at the driver, the jeep jerked forward and soon we were traveling at a good speed. I studied the back of the lieutenant's head. I didn't dare look directly at the man to my left whose presence seemed larger than life.

"So, young lady, what is your name?" a deep voice questioned me in German. I knew a small bit of German but hesitated to use it with this man. My poor grammar might give him the wrong impression of my intelligence.

"Imbi," I said simply. "And yours?"

He laughed. "You can call me General. That is sufficient."

I sat. I had watched the young lieutenant place my small bag in the rear of the vehicle and it gave me a sense that they would accommodate me in a very civil way. Still, this man was very tall and his voice, deep, almost booming with energy, gave me a moment or two of feeling very small and unprotected. I had a sudden desire to get out and walk the entire road to Mahu if necessary.

"Would you like some?" the general asked and I saw his hand offering me a small square of sugar. At Father's we hadn't been able to get sugar for weeks. In Narva, not at all in recent memory. I hesitated, holding back my pleasure at the offer, thoughts of German soldiers eating sugar cubes, Estonian sugar cubes while my people drank tea or coffee with only milk if we could even find that, entered my consciousness. I knew better than to express this to him however, so I accepted the small kindness with another polite thank-you and took the sugar into my hand. Immediately, I wanted to tuck it somewhere, like a pocket or a purse so I could present it to Grandmother Olga or Aunt Ellen when I arrived. It certainly wasn't enough for a cake, but perhaps a cup of sweetened tea or coffee.

"Don't you like sugar?" asked the general.

"Yes," I said.

"Well, go ahead. Put it in your mouth and let it melt," he said. "I won't ask you to speak while you enjoy it. It's a treat. Go ahead."

So I did. I turned my eyes toward the front, watching the road rush toward us, feeling the vibration of the jeep's engine and the slight bounce as the tires encountered small bumps in the pavement. I let the sugar sit there on my tongue, refusing to hasten its disintegration into liquid by chewing or any movement of my tongue whatsoever. It was delicious, pure sweetness like life before the day the cattle cars arrived in Viivikond. It brought gooseberries to mind, the sweet jam we preserved in Narva, the strawberries I would find once this long ride was over and I was again barefoot with Kaaritas, juice staining our fingers and mouths at the farm where all the turmoil seemed to fade into vague shadows, where life went on and the only hiding was in games, where there were no loud noises, only the music of Aunt Ellen's songs and the birds.

The world changes. Sometimes we change it. Sometimes things beyond our power change it. But in the midst of the trials, there are opportunities for little bits of remembrance, for little bits of happiness, for kindness that breeds moments of peace even in wartime. That little cube of sugar melted; I lolled it around so the pleasure spread, delayed swallowing until I knew my saliva would leak through my lips if I did not. Then, I came back to the present, to the smooth seat under my legs, and to the general who allowed my quiet enjoyment without interfering.

"Thank-you," I said for the third time.

"Where are you going?" His deep voice was quieter now. His smile had softened it.

"To my grandmother's farm," I said. "In Mahu."

"Where did you learn to speak German?" he asked. "You are not German, are you?"

I gave him the long version of my family's history, of my grandfather's work as a blacksmith on a German manor, of my Uncle Leonhard's service to our country, of our land, our family, all the many details he perhaps did not expect but he apparently enjoyed hearing. He asked me many questions. I relaxed. I answered him. I told him of my mother's months in hiding and how we were together again.

"So, it was a great relief to your family when we arrived, no?" he asked.

"Yes," I said. Then I explained how my father had been arrested and imprisoned and was released only after the Russians fled because they knew the German army was advancing.

"So, Imbi," he said. "Why are you traveling this road alone like a gypsy?"

"A gypsy?" I laughed. I didn't answer him. How could I? Could I explain that my family was big and my traveling back and forth created a connection between them that might not otherwise remain intact? Of course I couldn't tell him that because at the time I didn't think of my gypsy travels that way. It was only later that I saw my movements as a sort of messenger, a necessary one so we could all know about each other's safety or lack of it. Of course, we still did not know of Karli or Artur's whereabouts. I hadn't traveled to Siberia or even to Leningrad. Still, I did take trips along that road, hitchhiking, alone, expecting a safe ride to my next destination whether it be my father's, the farm or back to Narva. My godmother, Liisi Tiitso, lived in Kunda, a town famous for its cement factory. I visited her often because she had a young baby with whom I was absolutely in love. I would go and stay a few days, help her with the baby and then continue on to my father's home in Kohtla-Nomme where Taavet would welcome me with hugs and kisses. Kunda, aside from Liisi and the baby, was a dismal town due to the manufacture of cement at the factory. Often the entire town was covered with several inches of dust. Still, at times, that was more tolerable than the bombs at Narva.

While the general and I talked, the road slipped under us and the Viru-Nigula crossroad came nearer and nearer. I recognized the landmarks. I pointed and said, "We are getting close. Wherever you'd like to stop and let me out would be fine."

"How far is it from here?" he asked.

"About seven kilometers," I described the rest of my journey to him. Then, in German, he gave an order, a sharp bark of an order to the driver who smiled and nodded. At the point where I expected to be let out, the driver made a sharp turn and picked up speed. I turned to see the general smiling.

"We decided we'll take a little side trip with you," he said. "I'd like to meet your Grandmother."

There wasn't much I could do except settle back again in my seat and utter another "Thank you."

"Well," he said. "Show us the way, Imbi."

And I was suddenly in charge. I leaned forward and pointed out the turns for the driver. The last seven kilometers went by quickly. And, as we turned onto the final, bumpy road leading to the farm, I imagined the stir my arrival was going to cause. What would Aunt Ellen think, watching a German jeep pulling up to the front door? Before the jeep had come to a complete stop, I tugged at the handle and swung the door open. The driver hit the brakes hard and I lurched out landing clumsily on my feet, recovering and running toward the door. Uncle Erich had heard the car, a sound not usually heard at our farm, and was already standing on the porch with a puzzled look on his face that changed to a grin at the sight of me.

"Imbi," he cried. "Welcome home!"

I stood before him, breathing hard, feeling a mingling of dread and pride that I was being delivered home in such style. "Uncle," I said, "I brought a general with me. A general who would like to speak to Grandmother."

"Vana," he called into the house. "Someone to see you!" Uncle Erich winked at me. "It'll be okay, Imbi. There's one of him and so many of us Vahters." Then he turned to greet the man.

Grandmother Olga appeared at the screen door and stepped out. I hadn't seen her for a month or so and she seemed smaller and a bit slower than I'd ever noticed before. But the light of her smile reached her eyes and she reached to hug me to her. A scent of sweet cabbage and potatoes clung to her, a homey smell, familiar and warm like her embrace. "We have a visitor," I said. "A general. I told him you speak German."

I watched her gaze move beyond me to the jeep and the tall uniformed man who had removed his hat and was bowing slightly.

I could sense that Grandmother was more pleased to see me than to greet this man in a German uniform. I was suddenly full of awareness that young men in our country, Estonians, some barely of age, just like my cousins Toivo and Eldor, could be conscripted by the occupier's army and forced to fight their war. If they refused they could be imprisoned or shot. I was not thinking of this while my general sat and chatted with me during our long drive. Suddenly, with him at the farm, and with Grandmother's appearance on the porch and her suddenly pale cheeks, I was flooded with fear. What had I done? I let my eyes dart here and there, searching for any sight of my male cousins. Aunt Ellen did not appear with Grandmother. Neither did Uncle Julius. But Uncle Erich and Grandmother stepped forward and politely greeted my general who shook their hands and introduced himself. I stood by, watching, and listening. As I look back on this scene, so many years later, I cannot recall this general's name. I remember his voice was softer when he addressed my family. The guttural syllables of German not quite so harsh as when he barked orders at the lieutenant. I could hear and understand most of what he was saying. Grandmother Olga was fluent in German. Uncle Erich much less so. Despite his seeming gentleness, my chest hurt from my overwhelming sense of responsibility and shame.

"Welcome!" Grandmother Olga said.

My general bowed slightly and looked at me. "Your granddaughter is safely delivered. She is quite brave to travel the roads alone."

Grandmother visibly relaxed, her shoulders less stiff, and a bit of color returned to her cheeks. I recalled our last encounter with uniformed men, when she visited us in Narva, in the streets, and the hurried way she would pass them on our way to the markets. She would avoid them if she could, but once required to address any of them, she smiled, adjusted her posture as straight as she could and offered a kind word. She did the same now. She wrapped an arm around my shoulders. "Yes, my granddaughter. Thank you for your kindness. I hope you did not go far out of your way for her."

The general shook his head. "I am assuming command of the coastline. Bringing her gave me a chance to know the country, the roads here. Mahu is quite beautiful."

Grandmother nodded. "Can I offer you something to eat? We are just preparing our dinner. We can make a place for you at the table to thank you for your trouble."

Much to my relief, the general declined the invitation. "I must get to my destination. But, perhaps some other time." He and his driver quickly turned the jeep around and sped away.

Toivo and Aunt Ellen came around the house, singing as usual, a bunch of carrots and handfuls of small onions between them. Aunt Ellen's sweet soprano, Toivo's newly deep baritone harmonized but as they looked up, the singing stopped abruptly.

"Aunt Ellen," I ran to her. "I'm here! Toivo!"

There was a moment of confusion. Of silence, then, reading the surprise in them, I did something that added to their surprise, I threw my arms around Toivo. Now I never before had given Toivo such a hug. Aunt Ellen seemed to not know what to make of anything at that moment. Toivo took my bag and my hand and pulled me toward the ladder to the loft where we all slept in the summer. He lifted my bag up and I followed him. Our blankets were lined up in rows, dormitory style as usual on the hay which smelled sweet as the dust lifted under our movement.

"Imbi," Toivo said. "Whatever happened that you were brought here by a general?"

I burst into tears. "I needed a ride. His driver stopped. They were very kind. I thought, like all the other times I hitchhiked, they would leave me near where the roads intersect. He offered to bring me all the way home. I couldn't exactly refuse."

My tears, my rattled nerves still raw, despite the weeks that had passed since mother sent me away from the bombing of Narva. "Do you think the Germans will draft you and Eldor into the army?"

My fear was in my throat now. Grandmother Olga, Mother, Aunt Ellen, Uncle Erich, Uncle Leonhard, they didn't talk much about it, at least I hadn't heard them, but their sons and brothers were gone for nearly a year and still no word had reached us of their whereabouts. I imagined Uncle Artur and Uncle Karli fighting for the Russians and Toivo and Eldor conscripted by the Germans, shooting at each other in battle. Or worse, refusing and laying dead somewhere. I had heard some things. All of the inconceivable fates flooded me now, yes, even that awful spectacle of the gooseberry bushes after the bombing. I stood up. What had I done with my carelessness? I must do something. Toivo was staring at me. I left him there in the hayloft. I returned to the front porch. I had no idea where Aunt Ellen or Uncle Erich had gone. But then, I heard singing. Aunt Ellen was back in her kitchen and she was singing. "Vaikne Kena kohakene (a calm and beautiful small place)."

And so it was that my fear melted away. I was in a small and beautiful place and in a short time I forgot my fears and settled into farm life.

Our farm became an oasis of sorts for the soldiers stationed in our vicinity. Not three kilometers from our farm was an encampment of the German army. Housed in a former estate, near the Gulf of Finland, a division of the German army had established a headquarters and a base next to the beach. It was their duty to keep a watchful eye on the Finnish Bay for spies or Russian boats. Many Saturday nights at our farm, in our barn, we swept aside the straw and dust, lit up the place with lanterns and candles and welcomed our neighbors from the area to come and dance and sing and share what food we all could muster. The soldiers came too, perhaps as many as ten or a dozen on Saturdays. I was the youngest on the farm, but my cousins Renate, Virve, Toivo and Eldor, developed friendships with the visitors. Renate and Virve, of course, being beautiful and in their teenage years, drew attention from the young men. But, there was no real romance, simply a lot of flirting. The only problem was the language. My cousins did not speak German but I did. So, there I was, in great demand by the young men who wanted to speak to my cousins, running from place to place, person to person, translating from Estonian to German and back. I was the busiest most popular person despite my mere ten years. Looking back, this must have been a welcome respite from the duties of war, for these young men, so far from home. To find a family like ours, full of music and fun and kindness who spoke a bit of German must have eased the burden of the war for many of them. Eldor and Toivo were not conscripted by these German occupiers. Maybe it was the warmth with which we welcomed them, or, simply because we could speak to them in their language, or simply because a small farm, so far north, so isolated from the battles that raged elsewhere was a respite from their own pain and hardship of war, but whatever the reason, my cousins were not drafted into the German cause. Our farm was unchanged by the German occupation, perhaps because food production was an imperative in a time of shortages of everything. I don't know if the Germans took any of our crops or livestock for their army. I know the Soviets collectivized all the farms after they retook the country in 1945. My aunt and uncles, who did not leave the country, as Leonhard and my mother did, stayed on as workers, employees of the state, for the rest of their lives. There was little left when the property was returned to the family in 1991; it is now used only in the summer to grow vegetables and potatoes.

I listened to Imbi's account of the Saturday nights at the farm, how the soldiers would arrive in jeeps or small trucks, sing and dance and play instruments in the barn and I try to reconcile these Germans with my knowledge of the activities of the German SS in other accounts of the war. The kindness of her general and his lieutenant reminds me that in prior wars civilians were protected by the armies, unlike the accounts we hear of today in modern battles where the television news reports disregard for civilian populations. Can there be oases of kindness amid the cruelty of war? Imbi's family certainly did suffer from this period of Soviet and German occupation, but this story leaves me with a sense that peace is really something we all long for, particularly long for when surrounded by the ruin of aggression. So, when researching the history of this period, I made several concerted attempts to identify which German generals were stationed in the area close to the Gulf of Finland during the German occupation of Estonia in 1941 through 1944, I could find no sure confirmation of Imbi's general's identity. The history of the German occupation of Estonia recounts a systematic conscription of able-bodied Estonian men into the service of the German army. It also records the transport of German, Polish and other Jews from lands west and south to concentration camps and extermination camps in Estonia, particularly in Tartu. Many German generals assigned to the eastern front of the war were charged and convicted of crimes against humanity, sentenced to prison or execution. A handful of them committed suicide after 1945. But, there were also many who retired into oblivion at the conclusion of the war and lived out their days peacefully with their families. We may never know the name of the man who showed such kindness to Imbi. We simply can acknowledge that it did occur and feel a sense of wonder that this memory of kindness endured long enough to share with the readers of this story so many years later.

CHAPTER 9

Imbi's general never came to the farm again. But, there was another army base at Mahu. After those Saturday nights full of dancing and singing, the General invited Imbi to the army base for lunch once or twice. Grandmother encouraged her to go. "Practice your German," she would say. And so, Imbi would get on her bicycle, ride the three kilometers north to the base and join the officers for lunch. The impressions, from her telling, are of a table set with linens and nicely appointed china and silver. She remembered the details in a vague sort of way, except for one thing, vanilla pudding. "I'd never had pudding before." Imbi's eyes, at age seventy-seven, lit up at the moment of recollection. From the way she described it, it was a sweet, creamy confection of smooth heaven. Each time, after lunch, the waiter who would disappear, then reappear and place a bowl in front of her with a smile and say, "A treat for you."

"It was better than the sugar cube. On at least one occasion they allowed me seconds," Imbi said. Upon my questioning, she could not remember the General's name. Regardless, Imbi remembered his kindness, his attention and interest, and the vanilla pudding!

While Imbi recalls the story of this journey home and this particularly memorable summer, I imagine the surface calm that perhaps would have endured through all summers on the farm with little distinction from year to year. That is how farm life is, so tied to the seasons, hard work but a sense of cooperation, with every family member knowing full well what is expected of him or her. The urgency of all the small steps of preparing the land, planting, maintaining, and ultimately harvesting and storing for winter. No wonder music lilted across the surface of things. Imbi sings for me the folksongs of her childhood, during our meetings as I record her story. I listen to the sounds, of course I don't know a word of Estonian, but I sense how the playfulness of the lyrics coincide with her recalled melodies. I suggest she write them down. "In English?" she asks.

"In both Estonian and English," I reply. I will include them in her story. She smiles. "It is hard to capture their meaning in translation. They lose the joyfulness of the phrasing, the fun." She recognizes the importance of what I am asking her to do despite the limits a language translation will impose on the songs ability to convey an intrinsic element of Estonian culture.

"You must see the Song Festival," she says. "Thousands of voices, all together. It is really quite beautiful."

I am excited at the possibility of traveling to Estonia to witness this beloved Song Festival. I will go, I promise.

"Every five years," she says. "That is how it was before the Soviets took over."

I make a mental note and scribbled this in my notebook. Imbi stands and goes into her kitchen. Soon I smell fresh coffee dripping into the pot on her counter. She returns with a plate of cookies and two elegant white cups and plates. We continue our session, and her thoughts go to the day, 31 January 1944 she and Lydia left Narva for the farm and eight months later Tallinn. Three years, I note, is how long Imbi lived with nightly bombings by the Russians, who, by the time she left Narva, had destroyed fifty percent of the city. Nine months later, the Battle of Narva destroyed nearly all the rest of it.

CHAPTER 10

Imbi continued to attend school, Lydia taught, and Lydia's friend, Amanda, who hid Lydia during the Soviet invasion, came to Narva too and took a job at the town hall. She lived with Imbi and her mother. Scarcity of essential food items went on and on and Imbi found it more and more difficult to find food even with their ration coupons.

On many evenings, dinner consisted of potatoes and little else. The gooseberry jam came in handy as a means to barter with others who would trade other food items for a jar now and then. Life went on.

With Taavet, 1944

The winter of 1943-44 was harsh. The history books attribute the success of the Soviets in pushing back the German army from Leningrad and across Estonia to the harsh blizzards, deep snow, below freezing temperatures and bitter wind of that year. The Soviets were accustomed to these winters. The Germans were not. Estonia was pounded with six feet of snow.

Imbi sat in the bright sun of her living room and recalled that winter with a shiver. "We were freezing," she said. "It was difficult to get coal. It wasn't easy to find wood to burn, so we huddled together, sometimes sleeping curled together for warmth.

"I got sick that winter," Imbi said. "I had a terrible fever and a cough. They said I had pneumonia."

Then, after Christmas, ragged German soldiers fled in retreat from Leningrad. Soldiers separated from their companies, lost, defeated, or maybe simply starving from lack of food supplies, were walking across Estonia toward the west. The German army was facing defeat in Leningrad and running out of ammunition and basic supplies. The men were abandoning the eastern front. They came on foot, sometimes alone, sometimes as many as sixteen at a time, some with no shoes in the deep snow. So many had such thin clothing that it was a wonder they did not die from the cold. I remember them knocking at the door. They were so young, teenagers, really. And they were exhausted. So tired. We opened our doors and let them in to spend the night. They slept on our floor. Sometimes they would bring wood to burn. Most of the time they just came in out of the cold and stayed until the sun came up and went on their way. One night, we had twenty-five men sleeping in the living room on the floor. We never turned anyone away.

In the morning, when we had flour, we made pancakes for them. We went to the cellar and brought up jars of our gooseberry jam. I will never forget the looks on their faces when they tasted that jam. Of course we had no eggs. We made the pancakes out of flour and water, and milk if we happened to have some. But to those men, they were the best pancakes they'd ever eaten.

She pauses for emphasis on what she is about to say next. "You know, we never worried about any trouble." Her eyes convey her meaning. "I was a young girl. I was barely twelve years old at the time. My mother was young and beautiful. We never worried about our safety. You know. They were so grateful for our kindness. And, they were nearly starved and so tired. They ate, thanked us, and they were gone. The Germans drafted boys as young as 16 into the army. The ones who came to our door were not much older than me. Most of them had been separated from their regiments, their commanding officers. They were searching for these, but all were in retreat, and, according to their stories, it was chaos. They came and came, stayed a short overnight stay and were gone."

Then, in January, 1944 a German officer in uniform knocked loudly on the door. Imbi had been in bed burning with fever for several days, coughing and weak.

He came with news. All civilians must leave the city by 31 January. Imbi, shivering under layers of blankets, heard him. She heard Lydia's questions and some hurried and curt replies by the officer. There was no room for negotiating or for compromise. A battle was coming. The Soviets were pushing the Germans back from Leningrad and would soon be in Narva. It was the duty of the German army to evacuate all civilians before the battle for the city ensued. It was coming. Lydia, Amanda and Imbi must pack their things, only as much as they required for survival.

Imbi lay in bed while her mother packed up a few small bags and as much food as they had. This was done in a great hurry with little time for planning, for thinking, for saying good-bye to neighbors. In the bitter cold, a long line of trucks, wagons, cars, jeeps and horses formed on the road west. The officer returned to Imbi's house and escorted them to a canvas covered truck. Lydia carried bags and food. A young German soldier lifted Imbi from her sickbed, blankets and all, and carried her to the truck. They lay her down and covered her with thick wool blankets and a tarp to keep moisture off her. "Still, I remember the cold," she says. Her feet and hands froze despite the many layers. Lydia hovered close to warm her.

Imbi described this night to me, so vivid in her memory, as she poured coffee and offered me sugar and cream. That winter in Narva, these basic items we ate in comfort in her living room were only obtained with ration coupons and only when a surplus could be made available to the civilian population. She recalled the urgency, the swift and businesslike manner of the Germans as they rounded everyone up and barked orders; the fear of being too late and not getting out; fear for the friends and neighbors they did not encounter as they made their way to the convoy of vehicles. A misery from the fever and the shivering and incessant sense of pressure in her chest from the fluid; mostly, the cold and the fear.

Uncle Leonhard left Narva for Tallinn at the same time. The truck was full of civilians and under the command of several German soldiers who spent most of their energy assuring that the maximum number of passengers were accommodated on the floor. Imbi could not sit up.

"I lay on what seemed to be a shelf, perhaps where the men who would usually be in such a truck lay down their equipment and guns. We were not allowed to talk. We huddled together for warmth. It took us three days to get to Rakvere junction. Usually, in a car, that was a two and a half hour drive." She pauses. "I know this because of my hitchhiking trips to see my father and my godmother."

Out of the tense silence, where the only sounds that could be heard were the purr of the truck's engine, the soft breathing of the people, her own incessant cough, and the squeak and creak of the truck as it lumbered forward at a snail's pace, came a familiar drone, high in the air above, then closer, then bombs and machine gun fire, then, sharply barked orders by the German soldiers to flee to the woods that lined the road. "Everyone! Get out! Now!" Quickly! Lydia and Amanda reached to lift Imbi.

"There is no time. Leave her." The orders were clear. Imbi was left all alone in the truck as the planes strafed the refugee line. "I was all alone. My mother at first refused to leave me. But they made her. The Germans were very worried about civilian casualties, you know," she says. I ask her what they would have done if her mother refused to leave. She frowns. "Who knows? It was wartime. They don't have time for people who break the rules during an attack."

Throughout the three days of this journey, the planes came, and orders to leave the truck were urgently delivered. Each time Imbi was left alone as the bombs fell all around. Then, when silence returned to the skies, the others returned. Imbi lay there, with the heavy blankets wrapped around her, with a tiny view of the sky visible through holes in the truck's canvas roof, lights of bomb fires flickering, and with them screams and shouts from outside. Or worse, utter silence as the planes flew off. She lay there, straining to hear the sound of her mother's voice among the returning passengers; she prayed she would return. Each time, she did with tears and quick assurances that of course meant nothing. Nobody knew when the planes would come again, except this time, it was clear that the planes only came during daylight hours.

With no city hall to hide them, nothing between them and the destructive force of aerial bombs, Imbi and her mother relied on their German occupiers to guide them to safety. For the three days on the road, Soviet planes came. "We didn't eat," Imbi tells me, "at least I don't remember eating. We'd brought so little with us. Even the small bags we packed had almost nothing in them. But," and she smiles when she tells me, "I had my Mishka with me." She laughs. "He was my teddy bear. Of course, we didn't call them teddy bears. But he was the stuffed toy I slept with and he traveled that dangerous road with me."

Finally, this evacuation journey ended and the Germans let them out at Rakvere where a distant relative, Aunt Pouli's (Uncle Erich's wife) sister Mannu, lived.

Imbi recalls Lydia knocking on the door to their house, being let in and sheltered. And, in some mysterious way that Imbi cannot recall, this relative got in touch with the family in Mahu. "It took a few days. Somehow," she says, "Uncle Julius came with his horse and wagon and took us to the farm. It was bitter cold. I remember the snow. I remember the road and the bumps and jostles and the fever. But, I also recall the sense of relief, the calm, knowing we were off that army truck and the Soviet planes would no longer be firing bombs at us."

This is where Imbi and Lydia parted company with Amanda. With warm and worried good-byes, Amanda left them and returned to her family in Sillamäe, the coastal town where she had hidden Lydia for those long months in 1941. Amanda survived the battle at Sillamae which was coming that summer and later married and had a son. Imbi did not know of this until the 1970's when she sent a letter and was delighted to receive one in return.

CHAPTER 11

It was late February before Imbi's fever broke and slowly her cough faded and she began to recover.

Life on the farm in the winter was very dull, she recalls. The farm was a place of freedom in the summers. This time of year, there was nothing to do. I was still weak from the pneumonia and the weather was still bitter. So, I was terribly bored. No school. Yes, a few books to keep me reading and studying. My mother and grandmother fed me hot soups, cabbage and potatoes. Lucky me, she remembers. There was more food here than we'd seen in Narva for many months. Very little meat. Here in Mahu Mother and I gained weight and I gained strength after the pneumonia.

Aunt Ellen and Uncle Erich's wife, Pouli, wove cloth during these winter months when there were no outdoor duties. Imbi helped them with the spinning of wool and everyone, including all the children, knitted with that wool – socks, sweaters, hats, scarves, all beautifully done. Imbi's mother was the seamstress and turned the cloth into clothing for everyone.

The battle at Narva began on 11 February, 1944. The Germans held the Soviets at Narva for eight months. Winter, meanwhile, had turned to spring and spring had turned to summer and life between the two houses at the farm returned to the carefree form Imbi had known every summer for as long as she could remember, but now with significant reminders of the war's encroaching presence. One beloved cousin was missing and this left a sadness over this warm and loving place of family and safety. And, from this sadness, Imbi overheard a secret she kept for the rest of her days.

The three years of the German occupation brought about some changes in everyday life beyond the constant presence of uniformed men. The river where Imbi and Kaaritas had so enjoyed bathing and catching crayfish had been dammed to harness the power of the flowing water and so the farm now had electric power. This reduced the flow of the water past the farm to a fraction of its former strength, and it wasn't quite the same experience she recalled earlier. But, still, they bathed in the river, washed clothes, and the sauna still stood in its spot nearby.

There was still picking and tending of the garden and Imbi's usual following around of Uncle Julius as he cared for the animals, only now, she helped. She was almost twelve years old. Strawberries, blueberries, mushrooms and hazelnuts from groves of trees in lands bordering the riverbank kept Imbi and her cousins busy. There were hand-woven baskets for gathering berries, and there was the actual making of the baskets to be done. Imbi recalls how they gathered branches of trees and treated them with water so they would become pliable, bendable, turned into the raw material for more than just gathering baskets. This summer, 1944, following the harsh winter and the scarcity of goods in Narva had left Imbi in need of a pair of shoes. Shoes were nearly impossible to come by, so Uncle Julius, ever the resourceful artisan, fashioned the thin branches from a hazelnut tree into a pair of sandals for her.

She wore them all summer and well into the fall, but by September, she was to say good-bye to her beloved farm for what was a very, very long time. Summer wore on, with its busy days, and pleasant evenings of song and dancing; she had no idea what was coming next. She did hear German and Soviet planes in the sky. The battle at Narva was not far away, and nearby Sillamäe, where Lydia had gone to Amanda's and into hiding in 1941 was the site of a prolonged and battle during the summer of 1944. By July 26th the Germans had retreated and taken up positions in what was known as the Tannenburg Line, which included the three hills south of Sillamäe.

CHAPTER 12

Imbi had once lived in Sillamäe where her mother had first taught school after her parents divorced. Imbi tells me, "They called Sillamäe the blue mountains. They were covered with wild flowers in the spring. I was very young when we lived there. I remember sitting in the grass and wandering, picking flowers and weaving them into wreathes for our hair. Daisies, and blue flowers called *sinililled.* There were so many." She saw the irony in the beauty of this place and what occurred there in 1944. This was the place of the last stronghold of German control over Estonia. When they were defeated there, in August, it was the beginning of the end of the German occupation.

In March 1944 the Soviets began their assault on Tallinn with heavy bombardment. The night sky was illuminated with fire. Imbi, on the farm, could see it from a distance of one hundred kilometers.

That summer, Imbi and her cousins, as they gathered berries or hazelnuts near the farm, could hear the drone of aircraft. She explains it, "We would be out in the forest, and we could hear air fights in the distance. There was anti-aircraft gunfire too. That was from the ground. It was loud so we knew it was close." She goes on. "We were so curious. Renate, Virve and I would be out picking berries and we'd hear a plane go down and crash, we'd hear the explosion as the gas tank went up. So, we'd run through the woods to look."

"We found burning planes. Sometimes we would see the pilot if he was lucky enough to get out of the plane with a parachute before it hit the ground." Imbi tells me this with a completely deadpan expression as she recalls the images. "Sometimes the plane wouldn't burn. It would just crash. We would find the pilot, dead in his cockpit." She pauses. "Right there in the woods, we would pull him out and try to find a way to identify him. They wore tags, or sometimes had other identification. We would take that so we could report to the authorities so their families would be told."

"We dug graves and buried them. And we made these white wooden crosses and, if we could, we would paint or scratch the name of the dead man into the wood. There is still, today, a few of these crosses at the farm, in the pasture where the cows graze. Our family still keeps those graves for those men."

She pauses in her narrative. "That winter of the bitter cold and the evacuation of Narva was the winter we lost Toivo," she says. "To diphtheria." There is a long pause. "He was sixteen and was to start at the University in Tartu. He was very smart and would have begun his studies early. He became ill and died so suddenly. He was such a friend to me. He'd tease me for being so small. But he was my protector too."

"Uncle Erich was his father. His sister Renate was three years older than Toivo. She and I were close too. We stayed close through everything. Many years after I left Estonia we were finally able to send letters. Since that summer, I kept a secret from her." Imbi pauses. "Uncle Erich was the only one in the family who liked his drink," she says. "That's not the secret though." Her eyes twinkle as she reveals this gentle criticism of her uncle. "He was sitting on the front steps one night that summer after we left Narva for good. And he was a bit drunk. I was outside playing or sweeping the porch, I don't remember. But, I heard Uncle Erich weeping. He was alone on the steps in the sun. And I heard him. He said, 'If God would come and ask me who I would sacrifice, I would rather give five daughters than one son.' I thought at that moment that he was so sad and missed his son so much he couldn't possibly mean what he said. He didn't have five daughters. He only had Renate. But he kept repeating it." Imbi paused in her telling of this. "You know," she said. "I kept that to myself. I never repeated it to anyone, until now. Of course I never told Renate. It would have broken her heart to hear her father say such a thing. Uncle Erich was in mourning…people say things they don't mean. I'm a very good secret keeper."

I nod and scribble this all down. She says, "The worst thing to happen to a parent is to lose a child."

"So, we weren't always that good on the farm. We'd bury the dead with very somber feelings," she says while a mischievous smile replaces her serious expression. "But sometimes we would take the parachutes from the dead men; they were made out of a nylon material. And we would bring them back to the farm and use the fabric to make blouses and dresses." She pauses again. "We were scavengers. We had nothing during the war. We needed clothes. You couldn't buy anything during that time."

I recall that Lydia was a talented seamstress. "No," Imbi says, "We didn't make them ourselves. There was a woman near the beach in Mahu; her name was Leoti. She was an excellent seamstress and my mother learned a lot from her. We took the fabric to her and she would do the work for us. I remember going to her for fittings. We paid her for her work with food."

So, the war was not far away despite the sense of relative safety compared to the three years of nightly bombings in Narva. The battle in Sillamäe went on through August. Finally, in late August, the Soviets defeated the Germans there. That, for Imbi and her family, signaled the beginning of another urgent period.

In September, 1944, Hitler recognized the German occupation of the Baltic countries was about to fail and decided to evacuate most of the German army and civilians through the Baltic ports, most importantly Tallinn. The Germans counted on the Estonians to provide the rear guard for this evacuation and encouraged the formation of a semi-independent Estonian government. This government was asked by the Germans to co-operate with the German military and to get young Estonian men to join the army. The Estonian leader appointed by the Germans, Jüri Uluots, encouraged young men join up, hoping this effort by Estonians would keep the Soviets out of their country, thus increasing the odds that Estonia would regain its independence once the war was over.

The main thrust of the Red Army into the Baltics was west from Leningrad through Narva. Their objective was to capture Tallinn, thus aborting the evacuation and trapping the Germans. In their way was a rag-tag multi-national rear-guard army consisting mostly of Estonians, but also Finns, Danes, Dutch, and others. The resulting battle, called the Battle of Sillemäe, was one of the bloodiest conflicts on the eastern front. The battle ended in a stalemate but prevented the Red Army from capturing Tallinn, providing the crucial time for thousands of Germans and Estonians to flee the country. Failing to capture Estonia through the northern route, the Soviets decided to take the long way to Tallinn and invaded instead through Latvia into Estonia.

On 18 September, when the Germans had already evacuated, the Estonians attempted to make use of the opportunity and formed a new government, headed by Otto Tief. This Estonian Government functioned for only eight days and at the end of this period faced the inevitable occupation by the Soviets.

The fact that the major resistance to the Red Army was by Estonian forces fighting on their own free land and not by the German army was of course not recognized by the post-war Soviet government and was the cause of much Russian resentment when the "bronze soldier" memorial statue was relocated in 2007. The Russians living in Estonia had been told that the Red Army had liberated Estonia from the Germans. The Estonians knew, however, that the Germans had already abandoned Estonia and that the invading Russian forces were fighting against the Estonian self-defense forces.

CHAPTER 13

Uncle Leonhard had held a position in parliament for the Estonian government. Being a prominent lawyer and involved in politics, he knew that it was time for him to leave the country. He had been captured and barely escaped execution by the Soviets already during the first occupation and he knew that his chances of surviving once they retook the country were slim. His plan to leave the country included taking Lydia and Imbi with him along with his wife, Maanja and her sister, Helena. Uncle Leonhard sent an urgent letter. "Come to Tallinn," his letter told Lydia. "The country is falling to the Soviets. We must leave. And we must leave soon."

During this last summer in Lauriveski, German soldiers still came to the farm for Saturday evenings of song and dance in the barn with the Vahter family. By September, when Uncle Leonhard's letter came summoning Lydia to Tallinn, the important question was not whether to obey the summons, but how. News was never easy to come by and fear had lodged itself in the family as the Soviets began to make their way again across the country. There was no way to know how far west their new occupation had progressed. And, there was no way to know if it was safe via train or the way Imbi had always gone, hitchhike and hope for a friendly and safe ride from strangers. The wrong truck could mean they might be shot on sight. The city of Tallinn was the target of Soviet bombing and had already suffered significant damage as had Narva. The solution for Imbi and Lydia came in the form of an army truck that was heading toward Tallinn. Lydia and Imbi could catch a ride on that truck, again one filled with German soldiers. And that is how it happened that Lydia and Imbi were able to make their way to Uncle Leonhard.

Imbi recalls this departure from the safety, or what felt relatively safe but was soon to change, with great emotion. "There was so little time to even get used to the idea that we would leave Estonia," she said. "Then, of course, we didn't know if we would get out even if we made this trip to Tallinn. I watched the truck pull into the yard. We were watching for it. It pulled in and suddenly, the idea that we were leaving was so big. I could feel that moment in here," she says, her hand on her heart. "I was, of course, going with my mother. There was no question of her leaving me behind. We had urged Virve to go with us and Virve had packed a bag and dressed to come with us. She was nineteen and wanted to go. She had spent her entire life on this farm and she was imagining that if she was ever to do anything, to have any kind of life, get an education, have a dream of her life come true, she'd have to go with us. Aunt Ellen knew that too. She wanted the best for her daughter, of course. Renate was not to go. Uncle Erich has lost Toivo. To be left without any of his children was too much for him to bear." Imbi paused. "Even if Uncle Erich said what he said on the steps that night."

"Grandmother Olga said very little. I think the idea of my mother leaving was just too difficult. Imagine, we still didn't know where Artur or Karli were. It had been three years since we'd seen either of them. And mother and I were going. And Virve wanted to go too. It was such a confusing time. The only certain thing was that mother and I would go together. There was no separating us. Then, in the midst of all this confusion, this not really feeling certain about anything, whether it was right to leave, or necessary, despite what Leonhard wrote from Tallinn, the offer from the Germans to take us on that truck heading west was what grounded us in the necessity. They knew things we didn't, or at least we assumed they did. And we trusted them. So my mother and I got on the truck. Then Virve got on the truck. But Aunt Ellen came running up and pulled her off. And Virve didn't fight with her. She just let her mother hold her, crying. Then, as the truck started to pull away, Grandma Olga screamed and tugged my right arm to pull me down. I almost lost my balance as my mother pulled me the other way. "Please do not take Imbi," my grandmother cried. "I will take care of her. You will be back in three months, won't you? And she watched us drive off with the soldiers. And that was that." Imbi's eyes were glassy as she told me this, reliving it right there in her living room.

"I watched my Grandmother. She just lifted her hand to wave. And I waved back. Then, the truck turned around a bend and we were on our way. We were to meet Uncle Leonhard at his apartment in Tallinn. Then what? We had no idea. We just had to trust him like my mother always had."

The truck ride to Tallinn was only a couple of hours. There was no refugee line this time. The road was fairly busy, but it wasn't clogged with wagons and walkers like the road from Narva.

Imbi and Lydia made their way to Uncle Leonhard and stayed with him. "The plan had been set by Uncle," Imbi said. "He had found a small boat. He had paid the owner a sum to take us to Sweden. We were only in Tallinn long enough to learn of this plan, to prepare ourselves to carry it out. Uncle's wife Maanja, her sister Helena, my mother and I were to walk past this one place near the water and see where the boat was hidden. Uncle told us to do this during the day to get familiar with the streets and the landmarks so we could find it in the dark. We did find it. The plan was to meet at five AM to depart. But, there we all were, Aunt Maanja, Helena, my mother and I, but no boat. So we went back to Uncle's apartment. What else could we do? It turned out that the Germans had confiscated the boat. We had to find another way out of the country and possibly another destination."

PART III

To Tallinn and West

Tallinn, 1944

CHAPTER 14

Uncle Leonhard's plan involved getting all of us out of the country first; only then would he leave. He stayed behind for reasons I did not understand at the time. Perhaps there was hope that an independent Estonian government could still manage to establish itself and thwart another Soviet takeover. Or, perhaps it was to protect us from being captured if he were captured.

Our second plan was to obtain a spot on one of the refugee ships leaving Tallinn for Gotenhafen, Poland. Previously, Hitler had ordered the Germans to evacuate Estonia and along with the wounded and all the others, lucky civilians could find places on some of their ships. The Germans took Baltic Germans, their own people who had lived in Estonia for generations, and others, so Uncle instructed us to go to the waterfront. We arrived at the port, the four of us, with small bags, almost nothing, just some essentials and food. The harbor was so full of people, all confused, all trying to push with elbows to get on a refugee boat out of there. The Germans and Estonians were fighting for control of the government buildings in Tallinn. Germans, Estonians, Swedes and Finns were all trying to get out before the Soviets closed the port. Nobody knew when they would arrive in Tallinn and when the shutting down of this only means of escape would occur. Or, would they arrive at all? The Estonian army was resisting their advance knowing the call by Hitler for an evacuation of Estonia by his army had been issued on 16 September. For all of us, it was a last chance kind of feeling. I remember waiting in the early morning hours, before dawn, with so many families, lined up waiting, hoping we'd be allowed aboard a ship. Eventually, we made it to the front of the line after hours of waiting. The first ship was nearly full by the time we reached the front. The officer motioned me forward. I stepped onto the plank, my mother just behind me where I expected her to be. Suddenly, there I was, on one side of freedom while my mother and aunts were on the other. I would be the last civilian passenger aboard. The plank under my feet started to rise.

"Imbi!" my mother cried. And as I locked eyes with her, I jumped off the plank across the blank space separating the dock from the ship, and fell back into the waiting crowd. For a split second, I watched, wondering if that could have been my last chance, but it didn't matter. I would not go without my mother. Whatever fate had in store for one of us would be for both of us. She hugged me briefly and we watched as the huge ship slowly pulled away from the dock. We were first in line for the next one. After another several hours, a second ship docked and prepared to take on passengers.

"We were relieved to climb aboard, finally, but we were also terrified. Rumors circulated and we saw Soviet planes pass over Tallinn out toward the water. Would our ship make it safely across? The hospital ship, Moero had been sunk, 637 people killed and we heard others had been injured through other attacks on these ships. Mother and I and my aunts descended a long narrow staircase and found ourselves in the cargo area of this huge boat. The floor was concrete. Eventually, it was packed tight with people. We were like cattle in there, but we were able to lie down and try to get some sleep as the journey progressed. I cannot remember everything exactly. I do remember sleeping curled up on that concrete floor. My spot was next to a pipe that was so hot it kept many of us warm. Except," Imbi recalls, "I was sleeping right next to it and in the middle of the night I rolled and burned my arm on it." To this day she still has the scar from that burning.

The ship was vulnerable. Soviet planes were flying across the water and shooting. The hissing and exploding could be heard as the planes soared past, low, dropping bombs, firing, but through those three days our ship was not hit. The navigators zigzagged across the Gulf of Finland to avoid being targeted by the planes. Torpedoes were launched and at least one ship was sunk with many wounded soldiers and civilians killed. Because of the need to avoid the planes, the trip across took three days. We carried some food with us but not nearly enough. Still, this ship was the first in several hurried journeys that brought us safely away from the threat that was storming its way across the country, the threat of exile in Siberia or worse.

This ship anchored at the harbor in Gotenhafen, the city in Poland now known as Gdynia. At the time it was occupied by the Germans. My mother and aunts and I left the ship with all the other refugees, and the place was overflowing with thousands. Coming up and out of the hold into bright sunlight, I kept close to Mother. It would have been so easy to lose each other. The crowds pressed in from all sides. Some spoke German, Yiddish, and many were Estonians. Of course, coming from the other Baltic countries were Latvians, Lithuanians, Ukrainians, all people who fled in the face of the collapse of the German occupations, who fled in fear of Soviet death camps, exile or execution or simply did not want a life under the oppressive Soviet regime.

In the port, members of the German women's organization, Frauenschaft, stood around at various places in groups and greeted the newcomers with warm welcoming smiles. The kindness that greeted us was overwhelming. We brought very little food and made it last the full three days. When we arrived we were so hungry. The welcoming women of Gotenhafen dished out cups of hot soup called Eintopf for everyone. The soup was a thick broth with potatoes, vegetables, mostly cabbage, but it was delicious.

There was no rest for us upon arrival. A cup of soup, a short rest, and we needed to find somewhere to stay at least for that night. Maanja had a friend from high school in Schwerin in the East German state of Mecklenburg. The plan was to find her and perhaps she would give us a place to stay. The harbor in Gotenhafen was in close proximity to the train station and we made our way there. The goal was to find a train to take us to Schwerin. We were not the only ones seeking trains. The platforms were filled with people pushing and shoving. Mass confusion reigned.

We made our way to the train station and as the trains pulled in we would ask, "Does this train go to Schwerin?" We'd wait and ask the next conductor on the next one until we found one that did. So many others were doing the same thing. Some didn't care where the trains were going as long as they were heading west. Every train was full to capacity and more. Finally, a train to Schwerin arrived. But we couldn't get near the door to get on. There were so many people on the train platform. But, I saw an open window in the car near us. My mother boosted me up and I dove in, right on top of all the people already in there. I was small. I could fit through. Then, I opened the window up all the way and one by one, my mother and Maanja and Helena helped each other up and I dragged each of them through. I was not very well liked on that train. Imagine, four of us coming in through the window and landing on top of all the passengers. Really, we landed right on their heads. People were shouting at us. Nasty things. But, we were on the train when it pulled out of that station. That's how we got to

Schwerin. It took us two days on that train. The tracks were so clogged, all who could were heading west.

Maanja's friend was not expecting us. Maanja had not seen her for at least twenty years. I don't know if they kept in touch through letters or how frequently they corresponded, but we went up to her house and rang her doorbell and when she answered, we just stood there. Four of us. Maanja introduced herself and the lady just stared at us. I remember the house was a... what do you call them... row houses? It was a small, attached red brick house with a small porch and five steps up. Her friend invited us inside. We stayed with her for at least a week. It was a very small apartment and she could not keep us for too long. But she helped us find our way.

We had no food. Our hostess had none to give us either. We went into the town and found a place that was giving out soup to the hungry. And there were many who were hungry. The soup kitchen served us each another cup of Eintopf. It had a small bit of other vegetables and a bit of fat to thicken it. To us, it tasted so good we didn't mind that it was the same meal twice in a single day. It was all there was.

So there we were, in Schwerin. We slept on the floor of our hostess's home. There were too many of us for her small house. And, we needed to find a way to feed ourselves. We needed to find work, or at least my mother did.

CHAPTER 15

My mother had a friend, a German soldier who came to our house when we were still living in Narva. He worked at a make-do hospital for the wounded soldiers brought there from the eastern front in a town called Treptow.[2] It was on the Rega River, not far from Schwerin to the east, in the state of Pommern, back the way we had come. She boarded the train again, and through his help she got a job working for the same hospital...a clerk's job. That was a very important step, getting work. Without that, we would not eat. The hospital was about two kilometers outside of the town of Treptow. It was a collection of ten two-story solid brick buildings on a wooded campus. The building had once housed the mentally ill. German soldiers who worked at the hospital or were in the area on other assignments lived there too. Mother was assigned a tiny room with one narrow bed. It had bars on narrow windows close to the ceiling. That's how we knew it had once been inhabited by the patients and had been a mental hospital.

I was not allowed to sleep or stay in that room with my mother. A family who had a small cottage on the property of the hospital invited me to come and sleep with their family. The other problem was food. Because my mother worked for the hospital, she could go to the cafeteria for her meals. But I was not allowed to eat there. It was only for employees and they were not allowed to take food out of the building. There was no way to feed me!

In the building where my mother was situated a pair of German officers shared the room next to hers. These two young men, Oskar and Hans, fed me. They were allowed to bring food back to their room in small metal containers because they were officers and had special privileges. Each time they took food out of the cafeteria, they shared it with me. This is the way everyone took care of everybody else during that time. I was eventually able to come to my mother's room to sleep. The family who offered to take me in was very large and they did not have much room. I ended up sharing that one narrow bed with Mother.

By the time we'd arrived in Treptow and settled in it was October. Mother enrolled me in a German school. I spent a few weeks struggling to become acclimated despite the bit of German I already understood. Because I'd always studied ahead I was well prepared despite the language difficulty. Treptow was actually in German occupied Poland so perhaps the German speaking school was for the children of the military families stationed there. Regardless, I knew more German than Polish so it was the best place for me at the time. From the hospital I took the train to school. Each day, I'd walk a short distance to the small train station, board a train that took me two kilometers away to this German speaking

---

[2] Treptow is the German name for the now Polish city of Trzebiatów.

school. This was an important element of my day, this passing through the train station. We knew the Soviets were moving across all the formerly German occupied lands. Here we were in Poland. They could break through the German hold and take Poland as they'd taken Estonia and the other Baltic states. Mother worked all day at the hospital so it was up to me to keep an eye on things in the town of Treptow and to listen to what was said at my school and report back to mother in the evenings.

We often took walks. The area around the hospital was pretty. It was wooded and we had arrived in the autumn so the colors of the trees changed and it was a pleasure to feel safe and to just walk and get exercise. On one evening walk, late that first autumn, Mother and I found gravestones deep in the woods -- lots of them. It seemed an odd place for a burial ground, or so Mother thought, but we'd buried soldiers in our pasture in Mahu so at the time, although it was a surprise to discover them, it wasn't a shock. The shock came a bit later. Some evenings we walked past the cemetery but at other times my curiosity got the best of me and we would go inside and walk among the graves. As we strolled one evening, I read the names on the headstones. All of them began with the syllable 'Von' which was an indication that these dead people were of the aristocracy in Germany. Our German soldier friends told us this had once been a hospital for the mentally ill but it was only for the very wealthy mentally ill. So there we were, wandering and reading the names. I then noticed that all of the dates of the deaths read either 1942 or 1943.

"Why did all these people die all at the same time?" I asked Mother. Perhaps there'd been an outbreak or something at the hospital that mother knew about. She worked there now, after all, and might have learned some recent history from those she worked alongside each day. But no, she knew nothing. The crosses were all lined up in neat rows, the dates so similar, the names so similar. We all knew of the flu epidemic in Europe back in the 1918 era. I wondered if the same thing was true perhaps only here and not in our country. The news of the world had been hard to get during the war.

There were others who walked in those woods for exercise too. Often, mother and I would pass others and nod and say hello. It so happened that one evening, as the light of day faded, mother and I wandered past the cemetery. An elderly couple (they seemed elderly to me with their jet gray hair and wrinkles although they were quite the brisk walkers) came by. I smiled and said hello. They nodded politely but kept walking. Maybe they didn't like our accented German. So many foreigners had come west from our country, from the other Baltics; the German people perhaps felt we'd invaded their homeland. But I had just been puzzling over the mystery of the dates on the gravestones and I said, "Pardon, but was there an illness here?"

The woman was very tall with a bit of a stoop to her shoulders but with vibrant blue eyes. She studied me for a quick moment after pausing on the path. She glanced at the man who stopped and turned as well. "Why do you ask?" he said.

"Look," I answered. "The dates are all the same. All these people died in the same year. I thought maybe there was an epidemic or something, like in 1918." I wanted them to know I was smart and knew about things, so I continued. "Like during the Great War," I said. "Surely you remember the flu." It certainly had to be true that they were at least as old as Grandma Olga who had told me all about that time when so many people became ill.

Mother reached for my hand and gripped it. I let her but glanced quickly at her face. Surely there was something this sudden handholding was supposed to tell me, but what? "Imbi," she said. "Your curiosity may get the better of you."

The blue-eyed woman studied the two of us. "Where are you from?" she asked quietly.

"We are from Estonia," I said. "We escaped just before the Russians got to Tallinn."

"How did you learn German?" she asked.

"My Grandmother," I said. "And at elementary school."

"Ah," she said, smiling for the first time. "You speak well."

"Thank you."

The man suddenly started to speak to his wife in very rapid German. So rapid, I could not understand a word of it. She responded just as rapidly and I could see they were quarreling. Mother still held my hand and pulled me gently away. We'd taken three steps when suddenly they stopped. "Young lady," the man called.

I turned.

"Who is the leader of Germany?"

"Adolf Hitler," I said.

"Who is the leader in Russia?"

"Josef Stalin," I answered.

"Good," he said. "Which of them would you like to see win this war?"

"Why do you ask?" Mother asked, a bit of tension in her voice.

"Because you are here in Germany," he said. "So, choose one."

I stared at him. "Germany, of course. The Russians invaded us. Your army liberated us from Stalin's takeover."

He scoffed. "You know nothing."

So I told him the story of my father's arrest, of saving Taavet, of living in the bunker by the river.

"So you are in Germany. Do you feel safe?"

"Safer, yes," Mother said.

"And you want to know why all these people, these hospital patients, all died in the same years."

I just stared at him.

"Do you?" His eyes glowered.

"Yes, sir." I glowered back.

Now he just stared for a moment. His wife looked as though she might cry.

"Hitler doesn't like weakness."

For a short second I nearly formed a response that might have given this man an impression that I, of course, expected that strong leaders liked strong people, but Mother's grip tightened on my hand and pressed me to hold my tongue.

"Physical weakness?" I asked instead.

"Any kind of weakness. Physical, mental, any kind." He too looked as though tears welled in his eyes. "So, young lady," he said, "don't let yourself be weak in Hitler's Germany." He pointed to the cemetery. "You might end up in there."

Hitler had ordered that these people be killed. Hitler had the mentally ill poisoned. And they buried them right there at the hospital, hidden away in the nearby woods, far enough from the road. Mother and I, for the first time, came face to face with a terrible realization that the German leaders were as bad, if not worse than the Soviet leaders.

"So many," Mother said. "I am sorry she asked." She smiled a doleful smile at the elderly couple.

"Don't be sorry," the woman said. "Not all of us are Nazis."

I stared at the gravestones. I tried to count them but soon stopped. We, I thought, might be sleeping in the same room one of these dead had occupied. I tried to imagine being taken from my bed, poisoned and left to die. I thought about Toivo who died of diphtheria, so quickly, back home in Estonia. But these deaths were planned, deliberately carried out. Mother shivered suddenly. "Time to go," she said, pulling my arm. We nodded quickly to the couple and retreated back to our little barred-windowed room.

"This is murder," Mother said "against his own people."

I lay awake, trying to see out the small window, trying to find a star in the dark sky I could wish on. I thought of Grandmother Olga and Virve and Renate and Aunt Ellen. I felt so far away, like I was in the middle of so much evil we'd never find a place where we could feel confident of our safety. What if Hitler suddenly decided to blame the Estonians for his failure to keep our country? Would he put all of us to death? I wished for home. I wished for the time before I knew such things. Little did I know, that first night of awakening to the wider horror of this time in which we were living, that more such awakenings were in store for us.

CHAPTER 16

Christmas, 1945 was coming and despite the somber conditions of our life in Treptow Mother and I were determined to celebrate. Snow fell and left us buried like the most recent winter when the German's met defeat in the blizzards and drifts along the Russian border in Estonia. Still, I decided that I was going to bring Christmas to Treptow for mother and me. We discussed the idea of returning to Schwerin to see Maanja and Helena who we had left behind with Maanja's friend in her tiny house. They were the closest relatives, the only ones whose whereabouts we knew. But, because Mother would have to work at the hospital on the holiday, we stayed in Treptow. Here we were, all alone, no family, we didn't even have a way to get word to home about where we were. We were afraid for our family back home. Sometimes families back home would be punished just to hurt anyone left behind by escapees. Fear of that often compelled Estonians to return to Estonia. Of course, with Christmas here, thoughts turned to home and loved ones. But, it came into my head one morning that I should make an apple cake, the traditional cake we always made in Estonia for special occasions. As I dressed for school, hungry in the dark morning, I thought of the officers who fed me each night. Not only would I make a cake for mother and me; I would bake one for these two kind men to whom we owed so much. I began to plan early since I would need ingredients that were not easy to obtain. I needed flour and eggs and apples and sugar among a few other scarce items. I was able to finally receive ration coupons so I could go to Treptow and buy food. Not only could I buy food, but with ration coupons, Mother was entitled to a pack of cigarettes with each month's distribution. These were valuable as a means to trade with others for the food staples that were more difficult to come by. I traded one pack of cigarettes for the apples I needed for my cake. This was an absolute victory for me. Fresh fruit was hard to get in those days.

Of course, we had no kitchen, so that was a rather limiting proposition. I learned, one day as I passed through Treptow on my way to school, that if you brought something to the bakery in town, they would bake your cake for you. Of course, there was a fee involved. This was the only way I'd be able to bake my apple cakes. Somehow, I managed to get two cake pans, two large rectangular metal pans, just right for my plan. For weeks I traded my ration coupons with others until I collected enough for the flour and extra sugar I needed, hoping my precious apples would not spoil before I had acquired everything I needed.

Mother laughed at my insistence on this plan. But she would be welcome at the hospital's Christmas celebration with the other employees and I would not. If I were going to enjoy Christmas, it was up to me.

I awoke before dawn again one late December day and in our tiny room with the narrow bed I mixed my flour and sugar with the two eggs I was able to get. Spices were nowhere to be found. I would have wanted some cinnamon or nutmeg or even a bit of sage, but ration coupons didn't allow those purchases and I had little money anyway. The store shelves had none of these precious items. First I prepared the dough for the bottom of the pan. Luckily I had found some lard so it wouldn't stick. Then, I peeled the apples, cut out the bruised parts, sliced them and lined them up perfectly as soldiers in a pattern. I covered the pans with some cloth to keep dirt away, dressed for school and gathered my books. Mother woke up and smiled at my effort. "Look out the window," she said. And I saw two feet of new snow had fallen. We already had a bit on the ground before this new white surprise. I pulled on my boots and said, "I'll get there." I kissed Mother goodbye and lifted my two cake pans. Then, rather than hold them straight out in front of me, I rested one edge of each on my hips so my hands could steady them against me as I walked. It was a two-kilometer walk to the town from our hospital home. As the sun came up, I followed my usual path to the main road lifting my feet high as I gripped my cake pans tightly under each arm while my rucksack grew heavier and heavier on my back. There was nobody else on the road. I was the only child living at the hospital so my classmates walked from elsewhere. As I walked, my arms ached, my fingers started to stiffen in the cold. I shivered. Doubt about my cakes making it all the way to the bakery crept in. Still, I stepped on trying now to prevent any more cold snow from falling into my boots. Of course, that wasn't easy and soon my feet were damp and my toes numb. This walk is thirty minutes on a clear day. It felt like I would never get there. Careful to place my feet so as not to slip and fall, concentrating on keeping the cake pans level and the apples with the batter inside, I trudged slowly, willing my arms to stay strong and my grip to hold out. Finally, just as I felt like my arms would give out or my fingers would freeze to the metal pans, or I would lose feeling in them and drop my precious cakes, I saw the bakery and a small stream of smoke lifting from its chimney. A few more yards and there I was, at the door, tapping it with one frozen foot.

"Come in!" the baker held the door wide for me. I stepped through and he reached for the cake pan on the left. "Your hands!" He cried. "Come near the stove and warm yourself."

The ovens were already busy and I could smell the sweet scent of baking bread. I breathed on my fingers as he took the second pan from me. "Don't spill them!" I cried. Then I laughed. "I walked from the hospital with them and I didn't spill a drop."

He was a short thin man with straight black hair and light blue eyes behind spectacles. His apron hung loosely and his baker's hat seemed a size too small. It sat toward the back of his head and I couldn't figure out how he managed to keep it there. "We will bake these for you?" he said it like a question. "Yes, please," I said. "I've got to go to school. Can I pick them up this afternoon?"

"Ah," he said. "Yes, you can. What type of cake is it?"

"I am from Estonia," I said. "It's our traditional apple cake. Have you ever had it?"

"You speak German well," he said.

"My family knows German," I told him. "How much do you charge to bake these for me?"

"Nothing if you'll let me taste it," he smiled as he said it. "Or, better yet, tell me your recipe and I'll bake these for free. That is, if I like the way it rises and the texture when it's done."

"I must save these for two very special friends," I said. "But I will share the recipe. It's my grandmother's."

He went behind his counter and lifted a small cake from under the counter. He cut a small piece and handed it to me. "Tell me what you think," he said.

I took a polite bite. It was soft and sweet, still warm and the taste of cinnamon filled my senses. "Delicious. Where on earth did you get the spices?"

"Would you like a pinch for yours before we bake them?"

So together he and I added a bit to each pan and stirred very carefully. I heard my train chug into the station and knew it was time to run for it. "Bake them for 35 minutes," I instructed.

"Yes, ma'am," he said with an amused smile. "I'll take good care of your cakes. I promise."

My feet were still wet inside my boots but I ran to the railroad station and worried about my cakes all day. Luckily, a bright and sunny sky greeted me as I left my classroom and started my return trip. My feet still wet, my thoughts on my cakes, I ran to the baker's and through the door. This time I heard the tingle of the bell as I swung the door open. "Over here," said my friend. "They're cooled and ready."

The trek home was much easier. Wrapped in a soft towel which I promised to return to him the next morning, my cakes were lighter and I was soon back in the narrow cell we called home. The apple's sweet aroma threatened to reveal my surprise when my German officers came and delivered my dinner later that afternoon, but they said nothing.

When I knocked on their door on Christmas, Hans and Oskar's eyes brightened and they kissed both my cheeks with gratitude. Of course, they wanted to share it with us immediately, but mother and I had our own cake! I must admit, that these were not the very best cakes I'd ever made, but to this day, the scent of cinnamon brings back that cold snowy day and memories of my friendly baker who so kindly shared his precious ingredients with me and my two German officers to whom I owed so much from this very tough year for my mother and me.

CHAPTER 17

My mother. Lydia. It's time I talked more about her. Of all her children, Grandma Olga was closest to Lydia, always. There was a quality about my mother that instilled in others a sense of protection for her, perhaps because she often had her thoughts in the clouds. Grandma and I knew her better than anyone did.

My mother Lydia, age 25

And still, it is difficult to pin down precisely what it was about her that left everyone feeling they needed to take care of her. It could simply be that she'd divorced so early and had me to take care of alone. Divorce was unusual at that time. In a family of seven children, everyone has their role, their place in the order of things, so she was labeled as the artistic, the beautiful, less pragmatic sister compared to Aunt Ellen. That helped her get away with things, I'm sure, because of all of us at the farm, my mother did the least amount of heavy outdoor work. But, she was the one to sew our clothes, to instill in me and my cousins a love of learning. In summer Mother brought to the farm every textbook I would be using the following year in school. I would spend the summer reading these from beginning to end so by the time we returned to school I'd already read everything once. The daughter of the principal had to do well at school, I suppose, but becoming a good student early served me well throughout my life.

In Narva, in Treptow, wherever we lived, Lydia worked hard and instilled in me a desire to do my best. I thought my mother was very beautiful. And, Grandmother probably imagined that she would marry again. She had a beau, Oskar, for some years until we lived in Narva. A very kind man, I remember, he seemed to be devoted to my mother. Most likely, had he lived I might have had a stepfather. But, in 1941, Oskar died of tuberculosis. This left a big hole in life for my mother. I understood that he was very ill and had been for some time. Perhaps she had become prepared for his death through the years when he was hospitalized and recovered, but still, losing him left her more alone perhaps than the divorce had left her.

CHAPTER 18

It was impossible to get word from home or to get any word to our family about our circumstances. We did communicate with Uncle Leonhard who managed to escape from Estonia and find his way to his wife and her sister in Schwerin. They remained there while my mother and I were in Treptow. Back in Estonia, my father and Elsa and Taavet may have gotten word that we had left the country, but only if Grandma Olga or someone else in the family got word to them. Their fate was unknown to me until much later and the final details of my father's fate were only revealed to me when I received some documents from Taavet in 2010. This is perhaps a good place to tell this story.

For the duration of the German occupation my father was employed as a manager of housing in Kohtla-Nomme. Elsa was busy at home raising Taavet who was three years old by this time. When the Soviets retook the country in 1944 it was only a matter of time until they arrested my father. There are, I'm sure, adequate explanations as to why he remained in Estonia -- perhaps simply because he loved his country and refused to flee. His arrest occurred sometime in early 1945. The details of how he was taken are lost. I know only what was reported to me so much later, the events revealed in a letter from Taavet who initiated some research into our father's fate in 1989 following a similar attempt by my cousin, Erna, Aunt Aliine's daughter who had appealed to authorities since 1957 to get information. I received this letter from Taavet in the mail on a calm, sunny day in Cresskill, NJ as I went about my daily routine. In his letter of explanation, Taavet included a copy of a letter from my father.

At the bottom of this message was a scribbled note of description that said: P.S. This letter was found by a railroad worker who arranges the rails. The letter was rolled into a small match-box and thrown out of the cattle train window as it passed Kohtla-Nõmme (where Rudolf had been living) on his way to the unknown. This note was in the handwriting of Erna, our cousin Helmi's daughter.

This is my father's letter:

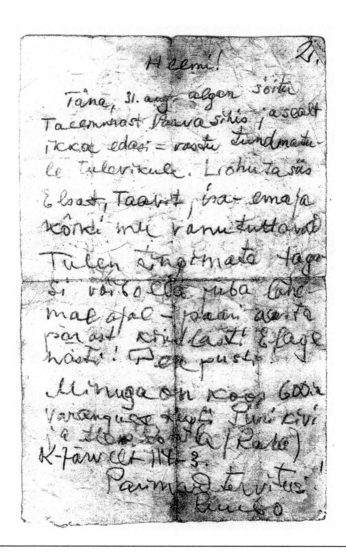

Helmi!
Today on the 31st of August, 1945 I am beginning my journey from Tallinn towards Narva and far beyond, an unknown future. Console and comfort Elsa, Taavet, Father and Mother and all of my old friends. I certainly will return in the near future – for sure in a couple of years. Wish you well. Keep your head high. There are six hundred people here with me from Varangu, Kupti, Piirikivi and other places. From K-Jarvelt 114.
Best regards,
Ruubo (nickname for Rudolf)

Accompanying the letter was this note:

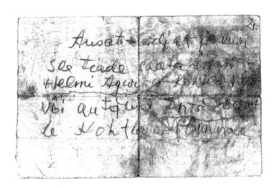

I beg an honest finder to forward this note to Helmi Agur, my father's sister in Kohlta-Vitsiku, or to the (truck) driver Ants Pomm at Kohtla- Nõmme.

Another note sheds additional light on this terrible period in my father, step-mother and brother's life. Dated 18 May 1945. It's signed by Elsa Peebo.

Fifth prison, Soviet Estonia.
Request:
Please accept this package for the prisoner, Rudolf Peebo, son of Gustav. Contents:

1. 2.5 kg bread (rye)
2. 1 kg wheat bread
3. 10 small pieroshkies
4. 10 fried eggs
5. 200 g butter
6. 100 g tobacco
7. 2 sheets cigarette paper
8. 2 boxes of matches
9. 1 kg cooked meat
10. 1 liter of milk
11. 1 piece of soap
Dated 18 May 1945.
Elsa Peebo

Rudolf Peebo was arrested in the beginning of 1945 and initially imprisoned in Rakvere. Elsa wrote this note to the principal of the 5th Prison, Soviet, Estonia and attempted to bring the package to the prison and induce someone to accept this on behalf of my father. Elsa was not successful in finding anyone who would take and deliver her package. Later, Rudolf was transferred to Tallinn. Taavet sent a copy of the note to Imbi in 2010. He'd held it since 1984.

We have no explanation why Helmi did not share my father's letter with Elsa and it was left for Erna, my cousin, to share with Taavet after Helmi's death. Perhaps she felt it too great a risk. Years later, after Helmi's death, her family found it among her papers and Erna brought it to Taavet.

In late 1945, Elsa received an official letter from the Soviet government informing her that Rudolf died of a stomach ailment. It is echoed in this letter Taavet received following his inquiries in 1989.

Soviet Estonia Federal Security Committee Investigation
June 27, 1989, Tallinn
Lp. Taavet Rudolfi p. Peebo, (Honorable Taavet, son of Rudolf, Peebo
200033 Tallinn, Ed Vilde tee 82-I25
In response to your inquiry we inform you that your father died 25 October 1945 serving his sentence for penalty at Krasnojarski prison in the city of Kansk. His death certificate can be obtained from Kohtla-Järve regional office.

After Estonia was liberated from the Soviets and restored to independence, Taavet investigated further. An official letter dated 26 April 1989 states:

"Estonian Soviet Prosecutor's organization has investigated criminal activity of R. Peebo. He was found guilty, 17 August 1945, by the Soviet War Tribunal. He received a mandatory ten-year sentence in a hard labor camp plus another five years of removal of his political rights and confiscation of all his possessions. Rudolf was accused of voluntarily joining a 'fascist' organization, the Estonian National Guard, in 1941, immediately after the arrival of the Germans. In Varangu, he organized a ten to twelve member group of the National Guards, owned guns, kept watch on the river bridge and participated in capturing partisans. During investigations and court proceedings R. Peebo completely admitted his guilt. His guilt has been also fortified by witnesses. There is no data available about his further fate. No burial place information is known."

Taavet learned that a 'stomach ailment' as cause of death listed on a death certificate from one of the labor camps really meant that his captors shot him.

Taavet and Elsa stayed in Estonia and lived under Soviet rule their entire lives as did so many members of my family. They lived with fear of speaking out about my father's sentence and death. It was only after liberation and independence that Taavet could risk sending a copy of these letters to me in the United States.

CHAPTER 19

In Treptow, early spring 1945, I made my usual journey to school each day. Mother went to work, as she did every day, at the hospital. I spent a routine day in classes with nothing out of the ordinary. Nothing, that is, until the close of the school day when I made my way past the train station. What I saw made me stop and gape. The train had been lengthened with the addition of an endless line of cars that stretched all along the platform, far down the rails toward the east. This was not a cattle train. This was a passenger train, much like the one I'd taken here from Schwerin. Smoke chugged from the engine way up front. German uniformed men scurried everywhere. Men in stretchers lined the platform, German wounded lined up for boarding, and pairs of men lifted each stretcher, one at a time, up and through the doors. I drew close. Some of these were sleeper cars, and the men were being lifted onto berths. Inside, men were doubled up on the berths, some of the stretchers, with injured men, were arranged across seats and held carefully in place so as not to fall.

Immediately I knew what this meant and without a word to anyone, I ran the entire two kilometers to the hospital and our narrow barred room where late afternoon sun cast a dark pallor over our meager possessions. I left my books and school bag in our tiny room, grabbed whatever clothing would fit inside a small bag, one for mother, one for me. I grabbed my Mishka and stuffed him in too. Then I opened the small storage box under our narrow bed and stuffed what remained of our rationed food and cigarettes into my bag and buttoned it closed.

I surprised Mother. I had never broken the rule about children entering the hospital before, but this time I simply walked in past the reception desk and found the small office where I knew Mother spent her days.

"Imbi," Mother said, "you know you don't belong in here!" But, she saw my face and knew this was not an ordinary day.

"Mother," I said. "We have to leave. We have to go to the train station. The Soviets are coming. We've got to get out. Now."

Mother glanced around the small office at the others at their desks. These other women were Polish and German. They did not understand Estonian. Mother's face showed her surprise at my rudeness. Speaking in our language in front of them was impolite. I should be using German. I had no time to explain myself.

"The soldiers are loading the wounded onto a west-bound train. Come see."

Mother refused. "I must finish my work day, Imbi. You are overreacting. Go home. We'll learn a bit more before we make any rash decisions."

When I didn't relent, she said, "Go on home! I'll see if I can leave early."

"No," I said. "We must go now. I packed. Let's go." I was not leaving without her and I refused to stay. She must have seen something in my eyes. She must have felt my agitation; my stubbornness was not going to relent. I watched her face. Surely she couldn't have forgotten our flight from Narva, our flight from Mahu to Tallinn at Uncle Leonhard's warning, the boat we missed, the stories we heard of other boats sinking, or families getting left behind because they didn't feel the urgency but trusted fate when they should have trusted nothing and no one. The bombs on the road to Rakvere. I could feel the echoes in my bones.

"Tomorrow will be too late," I said with a firmness that surprised me. "They are loading the wounded. Go look. Just look. We shouldn't wait. We should start now." With that, she stood up. She took her purse and coat and followed me out. She took my hand. I tightened mine around hers and we ran. Back down the road to Treptow, we hurried. The train seemed longer than it had just a short while ago. I approached the closest car.

"May we get on?" I asked. The soldiers shook their heads. "Wounded soldiers only. Civilian trains come tomorrow."

I moved without hesitation to the next car. "Wounded only," said the next officer. And so, it continued.

"See? They will take the army first. Civilians have to wait," Mother said.

I ignored her. Car by car, with Mother's hand tightly held in mine, I moved up the long line of the train. Each time, I met with the same response. My mind raced. Surely one, someone would break the rules and let us on. I thought of our friends, Hans and Oskar, the two officers who fed me every day. Surely, if we found them, we'd meet with success. But they were nowhere to be found. I was running out of train cars. No. No. No. No. I asked Mother to stay put on the platform as I ran towards the locomotive.

And there I stood, with the engineer before me. The only chance left. "Please, sir, may we get in and go with you?" I said in my best German.

"Little girl," he said. "You want to get me in trouble? I cannot go against orders. No civilians. Only the wounded allowed."

I reached into the bag I had slung over my shoulder. Without much further thought, I pulled two packages of cigarettes out of the bag and held them out. "Please, we must get on the train."

He looked at my offering. He studied my face, then glanced quickly at my mother standing further away. He reached out his hand and took the cigarettes and winked as an approval. I ran to Mother, grabbed our bags and said, "A miracle has happened." I climbed aboard and she followed right behind me.

"Imbi," mother said, looking at the only place for us, the coal pile. "I do think we would be fine if we waited until tomorrow and took a civilian train."

I climbed up and sat on top. I didn't answer my mother. I knew it was happening again. Even if she didn't understand, she recognized the resolve in my face and let me lead her. My father's words from long ago echoed in my head. "You are in charge Imbi. You are head of the household."

We spent the next eight days in that train, four days sitting on coal, four in a regular car. The westbound train tracks were clogged. Everyone in occupied Poland, including the Poles, fled in front of the Soviet advance. Our food ran out before the journey ended. The engineer smoked both packs of cigarettes. There was one train station, Stettin, through which all trains from occupied Poland must travel to enter the rest of Germany and there were only two rail lines across to the west from that port city. We knew we had to get through there. So did every other westbound train. News was mixed. We had no knowledge of the resistance to the Soviets as they overran Poland. We expected to be bombed, because this was a military train, to be boarded by Soviet soldiers and shot. We also knew we had broken faith with the Germans by stowing away and if anyone with authority found us hiding here atop the coal pile we could be ushered off and left anywhere en route to Stettin. Eight exhausting days later, after our train crawled along at an excruciatingly slow pace, we approached Stettin. Slowly, with a tension as well as coal dust choking us and drying our throats, we slid through the Stettin station and onto German soil. Our train was the last train and only train out of Treptow. Thousands of the wounded were captured and shot by the Russians who had reached very close to the town as we were trying in desperation to leave. Those two packs of cigarettes saved our lives!

PART IV

DP and Transit Camps

Displaced Persons being assigned living quarters. A somewhat befuddled
American officer is on the far left.

CHAPTER 20

We were on German soil. Mother and I were in a new and unfamiliar place surrounded by other refugees, greeted by Fraunshaft, the kind German women with soup for all of us. We pondered our next move. We knew Maanja was in Schwerin where we had left her waiting and expecting Uncle Leonhard to join her if he was able to get out of Estonia. There was a possible solution. Try to find our way there again. And this is exactly what we attempted to do.

As we stepped off the train in Schwerin, filthy and dazed, and made our way to Maanja, we saw the results of bombings. This was not a safe place. We were delighted at the sight of Maanja, Helena and Uncle Leonhard but Mother and he agreed we should not stay here. And there was barely room with Maanja's friend. Our short stay with them brought with it the same nightly vigil in the safe cellar of the city hall as we experienced in Narva. This time the bombing was from Allied planes, the same ones who destroyed Hamburg, Dresden and other German cities.

Uncle Leonhard was the only one among us unperturbed by the bombs. He was exasperating. One evening Maanja, Helena, Mother and I stood at the door with our coats buttoned against the cold, preparing to make our way to the city hall cellar as we anticipated the nightly bombs. Uncle Leonhard had retired early to bed to read a political article in a French newspaper. Aunt Maanja called to him and called to him repeatedly to get up and come with us. As we waited, growing impatient, Uncle laughed at us. "Why are you all standing there at the door in your coats?" he asked. He began to read out loud to us in French. We all went to his bedroom and there he was, lying there in his striped pajamas, glasses perched on his nose, with a smile on his face. Here we were, worried. The bombing had already started. "Relax," he said. "We are safer in here than in the street running to town hall." He was right. We suddenly looked like the foolish ones, all bundled up and ready to run. One by one, we all took off our coats, huddled together and prayed the candle by which Uncle Leonhard read was not visible to the pilots and gunners above us.

Mother found other employees from the hospital in Treptow here in Schwerin. Some had accompanied the wounded on the cars our engineer had dragged along as he smoked those precious cigarettes. They were under instruction, once the wounded had been attended to and transferred elsewhere, to report to a small schoolhouse in Wolfenbüttel until a decision or plan could be made for us. So, although we were two unexpected hospital employees, or at least Mother was, we took our place along with the others, nurses, orderlies, doctors, other medical personnel. We boarded a train that would take us to Wolfenbüttel to the south. Everyone on our train car was from Treptow, from the hospital; there was comfort in being with familiar faces and having a sense that there was a plan to protect us. Surely we were vulnerable to arrest by the advancing Soviets because we had been employed by the German hospital and that would be considered collaboration with their enemy. We could be arrested or shot on sight if any of us revealed the slightest involvement with the Germans.

We had already been traveling for eight days, with little food, very little water, no showers, no change of clothes, no idea what lay ahead and barely any sleep. Even after our short rest with Uncle and Maanja we were probably as easy to lead as sheep, so exhausted and ignorant of this place, and cut off from news from any reliable source. And here we were, on a train to another unknown place. Wolftenbüttel. All we knew was that it was toward the south.

The train moved a bit more swiftly than our sluggish journey through Stettin. Still, in our desire to get to a place where we hoped for a hot meal, a bath, a soft bed, the train ride was not nearly fast enough. Suddenly, an hour into our journey, we felt the train slow and come to a stop. We heard curt shouts and strained our necks to look out the windows. Mother and I, sitting, my head resting on her shoulder, hers leaning against the wall and window, tried to make sense of this sudden interruption of our journey. We surely had not arrived. We were not in a station. We were out in the middle of a field, with a forest to the east, a dusty sky with gray clouds predicting no good fortune for us as the wheels squealed to a stop. Clanking and some lurching of our train car, movement, slow movement backwards, then forward again, giving a quick but brief sense of relief that we'd move again toward our destination, we came to another halt and felt a vibration, saw the rest of our train pull away, and there we were, left on a side rail, in the middle of nowhere, with nobody explaining anything at all.

Our train car sat there for three full days. Later, we learned we were near Ludwigseust.

We received no information at all about why, about where we were, about when we might move. Should we abandon the train car? Should we scatter? Was there a plan to come get us? Why had we been left? Three days, three nights, without knowing where we were, where the nearest town might be, the decision was that we would stick together, we would be safer that way, we could protect each other better as a group. And so, we waited. I slept high up in the luggage net strung across above our seats where I could fit nicely, being short and one of the few children. Moving there left more room for Mother to stretch out for sleep. What little food we had, we shared. We all remained calm, at least on the surface, knowing how vulnerable we might be, to anything our imaginations could conjure. I lay on my net luggage holder, remembering the long refugee lines, the truck from Narva to Rakvere, the planes and bombs, sharp shouts to evacuate, waiting, rigid in the dark, holding Mishka, assuring myself I could tell my mother's breathing from the other sleeping adults below me. Yes, I was more secure, I told myself, than I was then, than I was on the coal pile from Treptow, or when I huddled in city hall in Narva. Out of the silence, the stillness, my net bed trembled just slightly, then more vibrations and more, and the sound of an approaching train, and it was upon us. I flew through the air, landed somewhere far from my berth, my skull slamming into the wall as a train made impact. Everyone was thrown forward, our stationary car suddenly in motion then rolling eventually to a stop, who knows how far from where we'd been.

There were shouts of surprise, cries of pain, of panic in the blackness of night, of despair but soon we learned that nobody was seriously injured. It was the middle of the night, in the dark; luckily the train hit at a slower than usual speed on this rail line. Everyone was jumpy, scared, demanding to know what was going to happen to us, if we'd been abandoned, fearful that gunfire or bombs would follow, groping around in the dark to find and identify each other, shouting for friends, for co-workers by name. But we miraculously kept our heads, stayed somewhat calm. There weren't that many of us, maybe forty or so. Mother bent over me where I lay on the ground, my head throbbing. I was a bit dizzy. I didn't want to stand up, yet the feeling that I must, that I must not be weak or show any weakness at all brought me to my feet. I remembered one important thing, and despite what might have been a concussion, or because of it, what I could remember was that Hitler killed the weaker ones, the ones at the hospital, and I resolved that I would not be weak. Not me. Mother guided me to a seat and lowered herself so she was level with my eyes and could check for concussion, but that was pointless since we could barely see in this dark car. Men boarded the train car and we heard short curt German words. Not Russian words. That was enough for all of us to exhale with relief. Someone from among our hospital group spoke up for us, a strong female voice, explained who we were, were we'd been, where we had been going when we were suddenly left here with no explanation. It was decided that whatever train had hit us would hitch our car to their line and take us. Where are they going? I heard whispered in the dark. I don't believe anyone cared, really. Collectively, we were just happy to know we were going somewhere as long as it wasn't back to Poland.

Mother wouldn't let me sleep. She was worried about concussion and nudged me into a standing position, so I held onto the back of her seat and rode through the night struggling to stay awake, shaking my head when she asked me if I had a headache or if I saw double, or if I felt sleepy. I laughed. "Of course I'm sleepy."

By dawn we slowly steamed into a station. 'Wolftenbüttel' said the sign on the platform. We'd arrived. But again we didn't know what that meant, what we would find here, how long we would stay and whether or not we would find food, rest and shelter.

What to do with this rather large family of hospital employees? It seemed we were expected but unexpected at the same time. The town was teeming with refugees, all of whom were ragged, in need of baths, food, drink and shelter. By the light of day, my head had a huge bump just on the top above my hairline but according to Mother, my eyes showed no sign of concussion. I kept reaching up to touch it to see if there was a gash or blood. It throbbed. I had developed a headache and longed for a cool cloth to fold and press on it. But there was little time for side errands and no time for weakness. Our group was instructed to report to the school house a few blocks away from the train station and we followed each other in a large rather disorganized blur until we saw it sitting there inviting us. It was so tiny. The door led to a small room, a single room where the desks had been removed. We were told we could sleep here until further notice. We would be fed at a different location. There was a toilet in one corner and soon we were all lined up waiting for this seeming luxury after what seemed like a prison in that unmoving train car.

For the local authorities in Wolfenbüttel who had directed us to our schoolhouse the first order of business was registry. We stood outside the structure, in a long line before a small table a few yards from the door. It was a simple wooden table behind which some rather severe looking men in German uniforms sat with large books opened to blank pages. We had all been employees and most of us could speak a bit of German so we were able to tell them about ourselves: where we were from, what were our names, dates of birth, education levels, how we had arrived in Germany, when we'd arrived, what was our reason for fleeing our home country. I suppose there was a risk of being sent back, although mother and I knew that because we had been in their employ and the Germans knew that alone would be viewed by their enemy as collaboration with them, we would likely not be sent back anywhere unless we did something terribly wrong. Mother quietly suggested to me, with an expression of amusement on her face, that I behave myself and bring no unnecessary attention to us. I laughed and with a quick hug promised.

The authorities directed us to prepare for several nights in the schoolhouse until other arrangements could be made for us to be transferred elsewhere or until local accommodations could be arranged.

The schoolhouse was much different from the ones I had attended in Estonia. Back home each school was a complex with apartments for the principal and some staff members. Here it was simply one room with a cold stone floor. Mother and I slept side by side with our new temporary family of forty. It was so crowded. We all gathered and surveyed our accommodations with a mix of gratitude and dread. Certainly there was barely enough room for twenty of us. But from among the men and women came a sense of co-operation – a true feeling of knowing we would have to make the best of a very difficult situation. We really had no choice but to figure out a way to make this work. None of us wanted to challenge the German authorities with a complaint or to ask for more than the circumstances were able to give us. We knew some refugees were still at the train station waiting for decisions to be made about their fates and they were very likely to sleep outdoors or under flimsy tents set up just to give some protection from weather.

Mother and I walked into the center of Wolfenbüttel in search of a meal. We wandered aimlessly through the tiny narrow streets hoping we would find a soup kitchen or shelter of some sort set up to feed the refugees arriving in wave after wave from the trains. Finally, we found a small kitchen with a line of similarly forlorn looking people. Each of us was given a piece of dark German bread and a small cup of soup. Against Mother's wishes I finished mine and got back in line for a second helping. "I'm still hungry," I said when she objected. The kind woman with the ladle must have had a soft spot for children because she quickly poured more into my cup and gave me a wink. "See," I said to Mother. "If you don't ask, you won't know." I shared the second helping with her. We made our way back to the schoolhouse.

Some of our schoolhouse group had already claimed some room in one corner or another and had begun to prepare for sleep. There was little else to do. But as we found a spot for ourselves, more and more of our group of forty returned and our spot got smaller and smaller as we tried to share the floor.

The light grew dim and evening came upon us. We realized unless we planned very carefully we would not all fit. Someone stood up. He was a tall robust man with a booming voice. He said, "Okay, we're a can of sardines in here, so let's line up like we're supposed to." It was accompanied by a good-natured laugh, a contagious one, so we all sat up to listen.

"If we all lay parallel facing our heads in the same direction, we can make room for all of us." And so, slowly, with a huge effort toward politeness, we set ourselves up in four rows of ten people each. Head to head, toe to toe, there was barely enough room, certainly not enough room for anyone to lie on their backs. We all lay side by side facing the same direction.

"Okay," said the man with the voice. "After a while, I will call out and we will all turn at the same time to the other direction. Get some sleep." He lay down next to the wall in the corner and I suppose he closed his eyes just like the rest of us did. Sure enough, I was awakened a while later to the call, "Links', it was meant as an order for everyone to turn to the left!

To the person, each of us obeyed. Goodness knows how many times that man called out for a switch but as the night wore on his voice became more and more gentle and quiet. Mother whispered to me that nobody would snore this way. "People snore when they lie on their backs," she said. We were so close to each other, side by side, a pack of sardines just like he'd said. After the third roll, I lay awake and listened. Soft breathing, a cough here and there, a bit of shuffling, but very little disruption to anyone, and not one disturbing snore all night!

This went on for a week. The floor was hard stone and turned cold at times if the temperature dipped. In the night, someone might need to quietly make their way across the sea of sleeping bodies to use the toilet, but they did so with greatest care to minimize the impact on anyone.

Finally, Mother and I were directed to the apartment of a severe looking woman who wore her black hair pulled back tightly from her unsmiling face. She was to put us up in her spare bedroom and it was very clear that she did it because she needed the money the government would pay her to keep us off the street, not because she was sympathetic or kind. Our room was tiny with a single bed that Mother and I took turns using. Some nights I would tuck myself into the bed for warmth and take up the few inches or so between Mother's back and the edge of the mattress. But it was so much better than the hard stone floor of our barracks at the schoolhouse.

Once we had obtained this housing arrangement the next step for Mother and me was to apply at the city hall for ration coupons so we could eat. The instructions were clear. Non-citizens reported to an office on the second floor at the city hall. Mother was busily making rounds to seek employment and to find a school for me to attend so it was up to me to make my way to the ration card office and wait in line. I was accustomed to this from my days in Narva and Schwerin and so I carried our identification papers and stood for hours to apply for our ration cards. It was an uneventful experience. I simply filled out the forms, submitted our papers and received our allotment of coupons entitling us to 500 grams of food per week. I left greatly distressed. Surely we would never survive on so little food. Mother came home and said very little about this condition. We had no choice. We were Ausländers, foreigners and all Ausländers were issued this paltry allotment of food.

Mother discovered that I could attend school and set me up as being eligible for a grade ahead of where I'd been in Treptow. But she was not able to find employment for herself.

During that week we met Aino. She was a young single woman in her early twenties, and alone. Her family was gone and she had escaped on her own, how I do not recall. She had found a place with a family in Wolfenbüttel and spent a lot of time with us. She could not find work and so I would seek her out and together we would explore the area surrounding Wolfenbüttel, which we were soon to discover was a beautiful town dotted with small parks along the river. Our landlady, whose name I cannot recall after all these years, said little to us, offered me no suggestions when I asked her questions about life here. She worked for the railroad. She sold tickets to passengers and spent any moment she could complaining about the ungrateful people to whom she gave information and sold tickets all day long. Mother and I avoided her wherever possible. She was not a very happy woman. No amount of friendliness or kindness or gratitude from us changed the hostility with which she regarded us. We stayed away from the apartment as much as we could when we knew she was home.

I walked the town. I explored shops, parks, the river, the bridge, the surrounding woods. I slowly walked past installations of German army, tanks, munitions stores, all the while thinking of home, remembering Grandmother Olga, the farm, and holding onto the hope that this war would end soon and that perhaps, just maybe, Mother and I could return to our country. Each passing day seemed to make that dream more and more impossible. I remembered Grandma Olga's belief that we would be back to her in three months time. It had been much more than that since we had left her. And each passing day I became hungrier and hungrier. We knew the Allied forces were invading Germany from the west. We didn't know if the Germans would be forced to give up their country or if they'd drive them back. I didn't care. I only wanted to return home, to have peace, to eat!

I was always a curious child. I paid attention to everything around me and so I learned that German citizens received different ration coupons. They were entitled to 1000 grams of food to our 500 per person. In my wanderings around town, I watched one day as our German landlady emerged from the city hall carrying her own ration coupons in her hand. They were a different color from the ones we received. I also noticed that she had emerged from a different door and seemed to be coming up from the basement. So, once she passed, I entered that door and stepped down to the long dark corridor. A line of citizens, all speaking German, waited and one by one their names were called and they received ration coupons. With sudden exaltation, I moved myself to the end of the line. As I waited, I invented a story of losing everything and arriving here just a day or so ago. In flawless German, I told my story to the young man at the barred window. In a few short minutes and after filling out some forms, praying that my ability to read German was enough to get me through completing these forms, I had obtained German ration coupons to supplement the meager rations given to refugees. I brought home bread, a few fresh vegetables, some powdered milk and six eggs. Mother was delighted but not as delighted as I was. We prepared this food when our landlady was not at home. This saved us from our daily hunger. I was still worried about showing weakness and becoming a victim like the men and women buried in that cemetery in Treptow. My weight was down and I felt tired constantly. These new ration coupons were my secret. I never told Mother where the extra food came from. She didn't ask. My father's words came to me then, "You are in charge of the family" and I allowed myself to feel proud of living up to his expectation of me.

Mother and I were very much aware that the Allied forces were close by. We also knew that Hitler was as guilty of crimes against his own people as Stalin was for his crimes against Estonian citizens. There had been an attempt on Hitler's life by men close to him. We'd heard rumors of death camps, labor camps and people who disappeared and were never heard from again.

I attended school and once every few weeks I stopped in the city hall to collect my food ration coupons. I was required to appear at the Ausländer office on Tuesdays, the German citizens' office on Thursdays. One afternoon, I appeared in the basement of City Hall and gave my German name to the young man behind the window. Immediately, he asked me to step out of the line. When I did, he came around and opened a door, beckoned me inside and led me to a small windowless room with only a table and two chairs. I waited in there alone while he excused himself. When he reappeared, the captain of the local police accompanied him. He was tall, wore his uniform stiffly but proudly and at the sight of him I knew my double gig was up. I'd been caught. It didn't take them long to obtain my confession. Yes, I was an Estonian refugee. No, I was not a German citizen. Yes, I was collecting double food rations for myself. I was hungry. I learned German from my grandmother. Yes, thank you I don't speak with an accent. I learned in school and I attended a German school in Treptow. No, I will never break the rules again. No, my mother does not know I did this. No, I promise I will not cheat the German people again if you will just let me go. And they let me go. I ran home. I was so frightened. And my mind asked the question over and over. How did they discover me? I had covered my lies well. As I arrived, breathless, at our small room inside our hostess's tiny apartment, I saw her eyes narrow to tiny slits at the sight of me. I nodded hello and closed the door to our bedroom and sat on the edge of the bed. I pulled open the drawer where I had kept our coupons. And right then I knew. She had snooped in our room and had found my double sets of coupons. I knew because I was so careful to hide them from Mother, tucked under my one warm sweater. There they were, my few remaining coupons, right in the middle of the drawer, uncovered. She had reported me to the authorities.

This experience shook me to the bones. What had I risked? Mother and I being sent back? Imprisoned? We knew there were work camps in Germany. I was thirteen years old by then. I lay on the bed and waited for Mother to return. How I felt that I had let her down, that I had let down my father, failing in my pledge to be the head of the household. What pained me most was my own failure to see the danger in my actions. In all these circumstances, all of our hardship, there had never been anyone who showed less than kindness and generosity toward my mother and me. We had joined forces with so many strangers, hid German soldiers in Narva, sheltered them, fed them. On our long journeys, Mother and I had shared food, shown whatever kindness we could, co-operated with those who shared our fate. I thought of the kind women dishing out soup at the train stations, at the port at Gdynia. And here, in our tiny room, we'd been betrayed by a woman who we'd forgiven for her abrupt and cold manner, a woman we felt had a heart underneath, for after all, she'd taken us in and given us shelter for which we were grateful. She had lost her husband in the war.

I learned that trust was not something I could extend to everyone. I had felt it in her coldness from the beginning, but I'd not really imagined her capable of this. I had to be more careful. For us to survive, I needed to not just be stronger than most, I needed to be less trusting, not only of people who were strangers to me, but less trusting of my own instincts for survival. One mistake could destroy us, Mother and me. I vowed I would never do anything dishonest again, no matter how hungry I was or how smart I thought I was.

A few weeks later, in April 1945, Mother and I stood on a bridge and cheered as British tanks rolled into Wolfenbüttel. Not one shot was fired in that town. Hitler's generals had surrendered. The Allied bombing of German cities had done their job. Dresden, Hamburg and numerous other cities were heaps of rubble. Thousands had died. This war was finally over. We stood in awed relief as the townspeople stood back and let in the British. Up on a tank, waving back to us with a broad grin across his face was a sight I'd never seen before. I hid behind my mother. Frightened. A man with entirely black skin and very white teeth! Mother laughed at me. "He's an African." And with a timid wave, I welcomed him to Wolfenbüttel and felt a lift in my heart derived from a resurgence of hope that peace was here at last, that the bombing sounds in the distance would cease and that Mother and I could go safely home. All of it was true but the last. We could not go home.

In Western Europe, at the end of the war, in 1945, at least 6 million people were displaced from their home country and unable to return. Add this to the 6 million

Jews who were put to death by the Nazis. Among the displaced persons were those who refused to be repatriated back to their country of origin for fear of political persecution, imprisonment or death for suspicion of collaboration with the Germans. Many were Jews who had been inmates in concentration camps, slave laborers and released prisoners of war. Many had fled, like Imbi and Lydia, in the storm of the renewed Soviet invasion and occupation. Borders were re-drawn and in some cases, the region of a country that had been home now belonged to another and so there was no real home. Camps were established as rapidly as possible and were most often under the jurisdiction of the occupying Allied military (French, British or American). Conditions varied. Food was still scarce, shelter was makeshift, often former army barracks, and many displaced persons suffered from illness, mental and physical. Families were in search of lost members and authorities established a system of registry, a central method of reporting your own whereabouts or investigating the fate of missing persons.

CHAPTER 21

Home was no longer a real place. Home was wherever we were together, Mother and me. But that didn't mean we didn't long for our real home, our country, our people, the lives we'd hurried left. We felt that every day, thought every day of Grandmother Olga, of Uncle Erich, Aunt Ellen, my cousins, my father, Taavet and Elsa. The war was over. The British rode into our town and crowds cheered, yes, even the German people welcomed them, as worn out by Hitler's war and fear as we were. We had learned by this time of the atrocities of the German SS against the Jewish people, against gypsies, the mentally ill. I believe all of Europe must have been relieved that the fighting, the bombing, the death would end. There was, I reflect now, a sense of shame among the citizens of Germany, for their leadership, and grim bewilderment, in hindsight, over how such a man as Hitler could have earned enough trust from among their citizens to rise to power and unleash such a force as this war. Entire cities had been bombed to the ground. The roads were clogged with refugees with horse and wagons, bicycles, wheelbarrows or just people carrying a few belongings and the clothes on their backs.

This was September 1945. What lay ahead was a mystery into which my mother and I peered, unsure of the fate again of Estonia but even without any communication with Uncle Leonhard, who had his finger on the pulse of power in our country, we knew, if Russia was an ally of these British and American victors, Russia would keep its hold on our country. The pressure of Grandma Olga's arms around me, holding me, just before Mother and I stepped onto that truck that took us from the farm, was a whispered memory of home. Her prescient understanding that I did not share at the time, was of the probable finality of that goodbye; I recall her trying to pull me off the truck, she knew that in all likelihood we would never see each other again. Artur and Karli, her two youngest sons, she had not said goodbye to them. We at least had said goodbye. It most likely was just as hard for her. Her final kiss on my cheek, her love for us, washed over me at times when the sky was dark and I lay under my covers, hearing my mother's breathing as she slept. Just now, knowing the night sky would no longer betray us with sounds of planes; the whistling of bombs and the thunder that followed. I allowed my mind to wander to similar quiet, long ago, and to again hear the real sounds of the night, crickets in the trees, a breeze rattling a pane of glass somewhere, my own heartbeat, calm, slow, steady. I no longer wished I could paint the full yellow moon black, but welcomed the sight of it. Would we go home now? Somehow, even with this new peace, I knew we would not, could not. The Russians had our country again. Until we knew the terms of peace between them and Germany, that return wasn't going to happen. Right now, in the present, as the peace settled over Europe, the victorious Allies did not know what to do with us, with all the refugees who had come to Germany for safety.

Mother and I were not the only Estonians in Wolfenbüttel. There were about a dozen. Our Aino, our dear friend, was here with us. We learned of a displaced persons camp being established for Estonian citizens somewhere to the south of us at a place called Hannoversch-Münden, Münden for short.

This was a charming and picturesque small town in a valley surrounded by the Harz Mountains. It lay next to the convergence of three rivers, the Werra and the Fulda, flowing from the south into the Weser River, which continued to the North Sea. In a park where we often strolled there was a rock in the river inscribed with a poem:

Wo Werra sich und Fulda Küssen
Sie ihren Namen büssen müssen
Und dort enstert durch diesem Kuss
Deutsch biz zu Meer der Weserfluss.

In translation:
When Werra and Fulda rivers each other kiss, they have to sacrifice their names,
To form the river Weser from their kiss.
That flows through Germany up to the North Sea.

At first the Allied solution to the refugee problem was to send every person back to their country of origin. Trains full of refugees took them back to their countries, but this policy did not take into account the danger of imprisonment and execution by the Soviets of those who objected to their occupation, not only in Estonia, but in Latvia, Lithuania, and Poland, the Ukraine, so many places. This policy soon changed.

We were registered with the German government as Estonian refugees, of course, since we had to in order to receive ration coupons upon our arrival in Wolfenbüttel. Now, under the Allies, there were no attempts to coerce us into returning to Estonia. We went on with life as we had been living. So, when we heard of the displaced persons camp called Hannoversch-Münden, we voluntarily made our way there. Again, a train ride to a new, unknown place. But on this journey we knew we were going to get help. The Allied soldiers shared their food with us, just as the German soldiers had done in Treptow. And, I have to confess, after the Allies were in charge, the coupons for food were double the amount for "Ausländer" than for the Germans. Maybe it was to justify the previous wrongdoings. Double was still barely enough food to survive and I had fleeting thoughts about trying my earlier trick of obtaining German ration coupons on top of our Ausländer ones, but I reminded myself of that hard lesson about honesty and quickly dismissed the idea. I would find other ways to survive.

CHAPTER 22

Imagine summer camp. Imagine summer camp lasting for five uninterrupted years. Waking in the morning, calling from the doorway of a tiny bedroom into the hallway, "Let's play soccer!" Doors opened and children emerged, and within minutes, we were choosing teams, together, outdoors, in the wide open field of what had formerly been a barracks for the military, a deep green field where we could play, unconcerned about the wide open blue sky above us except to gaze up and savor its beauty and the warmth of the sun shining down and browning our skin. We, the teenagers of Hannoversch-Münden, enjoyed a life that included minimal chores. We had no homes to clean, no grocery lines to stand in for hours with ration coupons clutched in our hungry hands. We had no jobs; there were none. For a while we had no school to attend. We were free to gather any time of day or evening, for games, music, sports, or to just be ourselves and enjoy the company of others our own age who spoke our native language, shared a culture and shared a tradition of music and faith and community. At our displaced persons camp we knew with an unusual certainty that we would be fed, at least once each day, a hot bowl of soup and a chunk of dark German bread.

My sense of responsibility for my mother was still sharp but, on a day-to-day basis, my father's "you are the head of the family" occupied less of my consciousness.

We arrived in September, 1945 by train in Hannoversch-Münden and walked two kilometers to the refugee camp. We had the clothes on our backs and carried almost nothing. Aino was with us. We had become a family of three. She was ten years older than me, perhaps that same number of years younger than Mother. A sister to me, as my cousins at Mahu had been. Together we approached the large two story brick building in a complex that included smaller structures, barracks that looked a bit like tiny homes, humble ones – shacks really. It had housed military but the Allies disbanded the German army and evicted any previous occupants in order to create the displaced persons (DP) camp. It was a busy place. Young children ran about in small clusters surrounded by attentive adults who seemed to be patiently, passively awaiting instructions from the young uniformed men managing what appeared to be a line of recent arrivals like us.

The camp was full of refugees before we arrived. Rooms had been assigned to families, barrack sized cells that might have been meant for two soldiers now housed entire families. Mother's last name was Vahter, her family name, resumed after her divorce from Father. My last name was my father's name, Peebo. Aino, of course, was not quite family so although we hoped we would share a place to live, this was more difficult than we could anticipate. It was difficult enough to provide proof that I was really my mother's daughter with our different last names.

"Do you have papers?" Mother had studied English for a few short years of formal school back in Estonia and could get by, but barely.

"This is what we have," she replied, showing them the papers issued by the Germans. Mother produced my birth certificate and her divorce papers as well as her marriage documents, by now yellowed and frayed. All the papers were in Estonian, of course, and the Brits could barely understand us in conversation.

"Here is the date of marriage, the date of my birth, the date of the divorce. She is my daughter. She has her father's name."

Soon we were directed to the Estonian authorities who were in charge of the camp. No more language difficulties!

They assigned us to a tiny house just a bit to the right of the large two story brick building. Aino came too.

Immediately, we set out with a borrowed broom and what we could find to clean with and tried to make our little shack into a home. There were families, three or four people to a room in the large brick building. We had no more room than those families, but we had windows and the fresh air of a cross breeze when the door was open, three mattresses on the floor for sleeping, and a small table. We piled the mattresses one on top of the other during the day and spread them across the floor when the sun set. I slept somewhere in between the two. There wasn't much else to our little home, but it was ours.

We found the latrines, the bathhouse, the kitchen, a communal place in a small structure to the right of the large house where the daily soup was served and where, if we were able to obtain other foodstuffs, we could use the stove.

Woods surrounded our camp and town and Mother and I found branches with leaves colored for autumn and cut them to decorate our tiny place. Vases were impossible luxuries so we used a bucket instead and created pretty arrangements to chase away the austere plainness of our quarters. Food was scarce and unpredictable, even with the help of the Allied occupiers. Most of Europe's farms were wrecked by bombings and battles, stripped of all yields, from the fields; animals had all been slaughtered for the troops and there had been nothing saved or planted for the coming winter. Mother and I remembered the saving grace of our family's farm and the fresh produce we were able to get when in Narva. These special resources were long in the past.

At noon on the first day we left our tiny shack and followed our fellow refugees to the kitchen where we were greeted in our own language by women in large white aprons with ladles in their hands, smiling and serving up what was to become a familiar daily source of nourishment, a watery soup concocted mainly of water and dried peas. We took a small cut of bread and a spoon and gratefully held up our bowls to accept our meager ration of soup. At least it was hot.

"School is our next step," said Mother, always the teacher. That first afternoon she went in search among the administrative leaders of our DP camp and offered her services. Slowly, as each day passed, the community in our camp formed. School started immediately, but only at the elementary level. Refugees continued to arrive, and as the Allies increased their occupation of Germany, more of the British army.

A knock in the door one afternoon surprised Mother and me. Knocks on doors were not welcome, as you can imagine. We'd had enough surprise knocks on doors since as far back as I could remember. This time it was two British soldiers.

"Pack up your belongings," one said. "You are moving."

They instructed us to report to the administrative office of housing for information. Quickly, we did as they ordered. Aino, Mother and I didn't have much, only clothes, a few pictures and books. We carried our things and walked down the hill to the main building. I was expecting to be told we would again be climbing aboard a train, moving off to some new unknown and place. It flashed through my mind that perhaps we were being sent back to Estonia. I glanced at Mother. I knew we could not do that. Father's ancient words, "You are in charge, Imbi" came to mind. I resolved I would fight if necessary, we'd run away, go find something else, but I would not let them send my mother back to Estonia to sure exile or death. Although, of course, imagining being back in our country, at the farm with my cousins, was a pleasant thought. And I felt some regret that I would be leaving Aino and the new friends I had made these last two weeks at the DP camp.

None of my worries came true. We were told the soldiers needed our little shack and we would be housed elsewhere. We weren't moving except to the brick building with everyone else. Where they would find a room for the three of us was a big question. They hadn't found one two weeks earlier when we'd arrived so it was unlikely they had one now. Many more people had arrived in the meantime.

Mother was assigned a bed in a room with the Haarmanns, a mother with a son, Udo and daughter, Astrid, but there was no room for me there. Next, the kind but firm man behind the table looked at Aino. She was added to a room occupied by another family of four, the Eichorns. That left me. They had nowhere to put me. The last name mismatch was still getting in the way for Mother and me. How to insist that we be together in such circumstances? I waited, sitting outside of the room where these decisions were made on our fate, worried that they would decide to move me to some other camp, that fate had finally and dreadfully stepped in to separate my mother and me after all our good fortune so far, when my new friend Helgi saw me. She raced off to her mother and came back in a few short minutes. Helgi's mother was a kind and warm person.

"Come in with us, Imbi," said Helgi's mother. I stood, feeling a rush of sudden hope when Helgi's mother said with simple grace, "She can stay with us. We have room." My worry was soon replaced by immense relief and gratitude.

And that was that. I slept on a mattress on the floor with Helgi and her younger brother Mart. Crisis solved.

Still, several times a week Mother visited the administration and repeated her request that she and I be housed together. I did the same. Life drifted on. Life was filled up every day for us, the children and adolescents at the camp. We had games, songs, free time to gather, play ping-pong, and talk, dance in the evenings. For the adults, it was a different experience. For Mother there was teaching. For many other adults there was little to keep them productive.

With Helgi in our Girl Scout uniforms

Helgi's father beckoned me one day. "Come with me," he said. He took me to a building across the way where the men built things. "Look what we've got for you," he said with a hint of mystery. A bunk-bed! "We can fit you in with your mother with this."

And so, with only a small bit of resistance that quickly dissipated, we moved his handmade bunk-bed into the room with my mother. It was a tight squeeze but the Haarmann family had no objections. Family was all we had left after these years of struggle and exile. They shared in our new happiness at our complete reunion.

There we were, in our room, five of us, Mother in the lower bunk, our Haarmann family roommates in their single beds, me up top. I was small enough and nimble enough to climb up there. But, that didn't mean I stayed there. More than one night I ended up on the floor, landing with a loud crash and a shout, waking up everyone from their sound sleeps. It took me a while but I learned that I was a very restless sleeper and that if I wanted to stop bruising myself and hitting my head, I must learn to be still in my sleep. There was no safety bar. Mother placed soft blankets or clothes on the floor below me just in case I continued to drop in the middle of the night. Eventually, I slept with stillness and quietude, settling into our new place with a sense, finally, of being able to give over to the new safety that was ours; bringing us to the peace that all of Europe was discovering anew with waves of shared relief. Mother and I were safe. That allowed us to live day to day, but we did not know if the rest of our family, in exile or back in Estonia was enjoying this same safety. It would take several decades for us to learn of their fate.

We were fed our one hot meal per day. In the afternoon the kitchen served the children oatmeal. We lined up and took our share, but with no sugar or fruit, the oatmeal was simply oats and water, a gooey mess that tasted of cardboard. We forced ourselves to swallow it down with a bit of extra water, knowing we needed the nutrition, not because it was satisfying in any way. For decades, I could not eat oatmeal after we left that camp. My appreciation for tasty food must come from those years and those tasteless bowls of mush!

CHAPTER 23

Mother taught in the elementary school that was established soon after our arrival. There were so many children. Young children. Classes formed, first with informal and then formal lessons. Not only were rooms for living hard to come by, classrooms were next to impossible. A school from grades one through six was established. Books in our language did not exist here in Germany. If anyone had a textbook in his possession it would be copied by hand ten times over. Sometimes the students would copy, other times older adults would be recruited and they willingly pitched in to help. A judge, an acquaintance of my mother's from Narva, copied a textbook for me and many of my classmates borrowed it to create one for themselves. A system and schedule was established so children could be grouped by age and ability, and lessons were created and given as best as circumstances allowed. Eventually, enough copied books were available.

I was thirteen. I should have been in what is the eighth grade here in the United States, but with a mother like mine my learning had progressed well beyond eighth grade level. There was no gymnasium here, the European word for high school. Still, we settled in. Mother taught and Aino helped our DP camp leaders with whatever they needed help with organizing, arranging, helping distribute whatever supplies arrived for us from elsewhere.

We had many teenagers but no high school. Forty kilometers away, however, was the university town of Göttingen.

Göttingen University, one of the oldest and best-regarded universities in Germany, was purged in 1933 by the Nazis of what they called, 'Jewish Physics'. Many world-renowned scientists, among them Max Born, James Franck, and Emmy Noether fled abroad and many who did not escape died in Nazi camps. When the British occupied the area the university began to come alive again.

We were very lucky students. Arrangements were made for the teenagers of Hannoversch-Münden camp to attend school in Göttingen, but the journey was too far for everyday travel. The teenagers at our camp, it was decided, would board at Göttingen from Monday through Friday and would come back to our families on the weekends. I lined up to sign myself up for enrollment.

"How old are you?" asked Professor Kilkson. He had been a professor of physics at the University of Tartu back in Estonia. He became our physics teacher but right now he was accepting our registrations for the gymnasium. He sat at a folding table with a wide book bound with a spiral wire and a pen in his prim hand.

I knew better than to tell an untruth after my arrest for my ration coupon escapade in Wolfenbüttel. "Thirteen," I said, raising myself to my full height which was only four feet and ten inches.

"Too young, you belong at the elementary school," he said and turned to the boy behind me who unfortunately for me was nearly six feet tall.

"I am not too young," I said.

"When were you last in school?" he asked, frowning, sizing me up.

"In Wolfenbüttel," I said. "A German school."

He continued to study me, and for a few seconds I could feel the doubt in his mind.

"My Grandmother taught me German." I said it in German to see if he understood as well as I did.

"That will do you well. Go to the elementary school and perhaps next year..."

"Let me try," I said. "If I cannot keep up with my studies, I will do as you say."

With classmates in front of school in Göttingen, British Zone. Note blue, black and white Estonian flag.

He softened and smiled. "Fine, you have two months trial," he said. "I will be checking your grades and your progress." He wrote my name and sent me along for a room assignment for sleeping and turned to the tall boy behind me.

It was a special place, that gymnasium. We formed a close group; thirty of us traveled together, learned together, roomed and studied and played together. It was special because the faculty of our school was made up of highly learned college professors with advanced degrees and had higher expectations of us than those who might have taught us under ordinary circumstances at home in pre-Soviet Estonia. The population of displaced persons at our DP camp and at Göttingen included several Estonian young people who had attended university back in Tartu and now they were continuing their studies at Göttingen. They were on average only ten to fifteen years older than us. Add them to the doctors of philosophy in many different areas and we had a wealth of intellectually gifted teachers who spoke German and Estonian, and many other languages. They endeavored to make up for the unevenness of our collective educational experiences during the war.

Our gymnasium was housed in Das Deutsches Haus, a three story building with our dormitory rooms on the third floor and classrooms on the lower levels. Every Monday morning at six a.m., I walked with my schoolmates of different ages two kilometers to the station and together we boarded the train.

We made up several classes, mostly by age group. Among my most memorable experiences during this time is our professor of chemistry, Dr. Kaho. Keep in mind that I was only thirteen years old in this chemistry class. Dr. Kaho taught quickly and we all struggled to scribble notes into our notebooks as he went through countless pieces of chalk with his presentation of chemical formulas on the blackboard. This went on for quite a few days. Most of us whispered and complained that we didn't understand a bit of it, but we couldn't challenge him and tell him we weren't prepared for this, especially me. The last thing I wanted was to admit something was too difficult. Professor Kilkson was often there, in the background, keeping an eye on my ability to keep up and he would surely send me back to the elementary school if I failed.

A few weeks later, it was time for a test. I studied. We all studied, but still, when it came time for the test, every one of us failed. Professor Kaho was stunned and disappointed with us. Of course, we were too. After Professor Kaho left the room, we all were disgraced; none of us wanted to take those test papers home to show our parents. We were upset with ourselves, but with Kaho too.

Harri, one of us, a slightly-built but very talented boy who played piano, went to the upright in the corner of our classroom and opened the lid. "Go ahead," he said, "put your test in." He sat down and began to play.

One by one, giggling, we did as he asked, dropping those failing papers into the box where the tiny hammers hit the strings to make music. Soon the only thing those hammers did was tear those tests to shreds. As the hammers did their work, the music became muffled until we dared to open the lid of the box and find the remains of our failures.

We were not the only members of that class to learn something from this failure. Professor Kaho learned that we were not ready for the level he was accustomed to at the university. He started all over again from the beginning, and after that we did much better. Somehow, that experience opened my mind to a new level of understanding and it set me up for a lifetime of interest in the sciences.

Classmates, second year of gymnasium.
Teacher front middle.

Professor Richard Harm gave me a solid base in mathematics, which served me in the future very well. We learned everything up to and including calculus at this excellent school. Professor Harm emigrated to the United States and joined the faculty at Princeton University as many Estonian and German scientists did at various universities.

We returned to Hannoversch-Münden on Friday afternoons to discover our families had saved rationed food for us. In the midst of all this activity, food was still scarce and whatever we received, we received with gratitude.

In our dormitories, we would sometimes receive CARE packages from the International Red Cross. Inside we found peanut butter, salty crackers, nuts, small bars of chocolate, some cereal, instant coffee and Spam. These were such treats that we'd eat the entire contents in one day, starting with the chocolate bar. It was Russak who came up with the idea of using the instant coffee, a favorite among the Germans, as currency. He collected all of our packets and took them off to a bakery in town. When he returned, we were delighted when he gathered us together around a large brown sack.

"Go ahead, reach in," he said.

Out came Brötchen, dark brown rolls, fresh and delicious, enough for all of us. Russak was a quiet and bashful boy. He was tall with red marks on his skin, not very handsome, but very good-hearted. He must have been liked by the baker. He took care of everybody, and under his constant expressions of kindness, we became a family.

The following year, 1946, all the Estonians at Hannoversch-Münden camp moved to Göttingen where we shared facilities with refugees from Lithuania. Our brick buildings were called Luttiche Kaserne. These had previously been used by the military but now housed our living quarters and our classrooms.

From 1946 through 1948 Mother and I lived at Göttingen, our longest stay of all the DP camps we lived in. I have wonderful memories of this place. The camp presented us with endless opportunities in sports, music, dancing and song. We were trained in track and field, and our gymnastics team of a dozen boys and girls learned trapeze, floor exercise, balance beam, parallel bars and rings for up to two hours every day.

My mother had taught in the gymnastics program for years in Estonia. A special class for girls, to teach us graceful movement and posture, gave us a lifelong respect for exercise, for strength and flexibility. The actual gymnastics team we were involved in gave performances for the Germans and our folk dancing group not only kept our traditions alive for ourselves but gave us opportunities to travel locally and to perform.

Song was and still is so very important in our culture and while we were together in this camp our leadership found many ways to keep our Estonian culture alive. In the evenings someone was always at the piano; we sang traditional songs and everyone joined in. I sang in a choir. And I was called upon to recite poetry. I knew hundreds of poems by heart because from a young age in school I had an ability to remember them. So often, even back when we lived in Sillamäe, which means I was only five years old, I had been asked to recite at events. I have memories of a huge hall with hundreds of people, standing on a stage in front of them all, and reciting a poem about a chicken and a lady who fed it. These poems lose their meaning and humor when translated into English but are great fun to share and perform in Estonian.

We were given religious instruction once a week in school at the DP camp and we learned religious songs as part of these lessons. So much memorizing in those days. We knew the words by heart long before their meaning was understandable to us. But those words are still with me today to share with my family. And now their meaning is simply Estonian songs and poems that speak of our home and our shared traditions.

These things tied us together across the many obstacles that stood between us and our family members who were beyond our reach. We were on one side of a great divide, here in Germany, while our loved ones were on the other side, the great barrier between freedom and oppression. Mother and I had originally planned to flee to Sweden but here we were in Germany with many hundreds of thousands of displaced persons.

Like most refugees we were still, as time went on, unable to establish a life for ourselves beyond the camp. We were still dependent on those authorities occupying Germany and we could end up anywhere. Much later we learned that the occupying Allies stopped sending displaced persons back to their original country after learning of executions and imprisonments upon their arrival home. The military war had ceased but the struggle to maintain power went on in the occupied lands to the east. We were in the safest place for the moment.

CHAPTER 24

Mother and I lived in DP camps for almost five years. Life was not just about waiting. Life at the camp was very full, at least for children and young adults. During the school year we received an excellent education. In summertime we spent several weeks in an international summer camp in Klausthal, in the Harz Mountains. It was established by the UNRRA (United Nations Relief and Rehabilitation Administration) for refugee children. There were numerous nationalities at this camp – Estonians, Latvians, Lithuanians, Polish, Ukrainians – mainly from eastern Europe.

Every two weeks the camp held an Olympics competition in track and field, shot-put, ping pong, badminton, volley-ball and more. It was extremely competitive between different nationalities and the Estonian team was particularly eager to win, most likely because in sheer numbers, we were underrepresented with 30 to 40 team members compared to the Poles who numbered more than 200. Despite the numbers the Estonians were always the winners in total score count. I did my best to contribute to that success.

Estonian delegation at the international youth
summer camp in Klausthal, Germany.

For the adults it was a different story. Their lives suffered. Those with formerly established careers, as doctors or businessmen or teachers, or professors, had no means by which to resume their livelihood. Professional pursuits were interrupted and for many, never resumed. I suppose my mother was fortunate that she could be of use in the camp as a teacher.

Frequently at first, and then, as time went on, less and less often, everyone at Göttingen would look for the postings from the Central Registry. These were long lists of names compiled by the occupying forces and our own representatives: people in exile searching for lost family members, friends, neighbors. We were on this list. We hoped to be found by any of our family who might also be in Germany or any of the other free countries in Europe. Every day, someone discovered a lost relative's address or status as a refugee. The list identified where someone lived and how to make contact. We would hear shouts of joy when someone found a loved one or if a piece of mail was received because they had listed themselves as residents of Göttingen. Mother and I studied the lists but for a long time found no news. Among those we sought were Uncle Leonhard and his wife and his wife's sister. We had last heard from them in Wolfenbüttel. Because of my Uncle's position as a former member of the Estonian Parliament, we wondered if he would reveal his identity. To do so might let us find him, but very likely, other forces might consider him a member of the government of Estonia in exile and seek to assassinate him. If he ended up in the Soviet occupied zone we knew he would never reveal his true identity and would most likely live under an assumed name until he found his way to the British or American occupied zones.

Finally, one morning, Mother let out a happy shriek. I ran to her. "He's here," she said. She hurried to a map of Germany that showed the zones. "Schwarzenbeck...where is...oh, here," she pointed. "Way up north. He's in the British zone too." His camp was in a town close to Hamburg.

We studied those lists for Uncle Artur, Uncle Karli, my father, Elsa and Taavet. Often we would recognize names of former neighbors, former classmates, former students of Mother's, grateful to see how many had gotten free, but as time stretched on and the addition to the lists dwindled, we were helpless to know the fate of many loved ones. I knew my father had been arrested once by the Soviets. I had no way of knowing if he and Elsa had found their way out of Estonia.

Of course, we wrote to Uncle Leonhard at once. Perhaps he had seen or heard news of someone. But his letter back destroyed that hope. He had also not been in touch with anyone we knew. And, there was no communication allowed with anyone back home in areas occupied by the Soviets.

To say times for families were chaotic is to understate the situation in Europe at this time. It seems the forces of the world could repair a railroad faster and sooner than they could restore family members with each other, no matter how much effort was put forth.

During the holidays Mother and I were given permission to travel to Schwarzenbeck. We looked forward to this with great anticipation, our only form of holiday or vacation during these years and our only contact with family.

Uncle Leonhard and Maanja and Helena lived much like we did, in a small room with simple furniture, a bed, a table, and chairs. We arrived by train carrying very little, knowing there wasn't much room in their small space for anything but us. Mother and I slept on the floor. So much talk, so many moments of laughter, such serious discussions of the possible steps we could take next, to find a permanent place to restart a life. I heard them discussing me when they thought perhaps I was busy with something else.

"She could enter the University at Göttingen," my mother said. "If they'll admit refugees."

"But she needs more than that. She's been a gypsy without a home for as long as she's been alive." Uncle Leonhard sighed. "She needs a life and a home."

But, possible steps were limited by what the authorities were able to negotiate with all the countries that would even consider accepting us so we could begin our lives anew. Uncle Leonhard kept track of the progress the occupying forces in Germany made with other countries that might accept refugees. Conditions changed daily as promising destinations either closed their borders or limited the number of refugees they could accept.

We might feel optimistic one moment and disappointed the next day as possibilities arose and disappeared. Finland, Sweden, France, Britain, Australia, South America, Canada, the United States these last seemed so far away. We kept on with daily life and allowed that vague sense of impermanence to recede to the back of our consciousness as we met the challenges of school and work.

At Uncle Leonhard's we gathered with him on Friday evening at the huge hall where special performances and meetings were held at Schwarzenbeck. Mother and I sat in the auditorium with all the residents while Uncle took a seat at a table on the stage, a thick pile of handwritten notes in his hand and newspapers in many languages spread out on the table before him. He was in charge of "The Week in Review." Uncle welcomed the crowd of hundreds of people, greeting them in Estonian, German and English. Mother and I had heard he did this. His letters had been full of news he had gleaned from his voracious reading of any newspaper or magazine he could get his hands on. His days at the DP camp, like they were for many others who had been in active lives in Estonia, lacked responsibility and so it was up to him to fill his time with useful tasks. Uncle read from the newspapers to the audience, stopping to consult his notes to tell which country's press had reported whatever news he was sharing. This was an every-Friday evening ritual. He sat and reported on politics, government, the progress of the Potsdam talks, events as far away as China, sports, weather, entertainment. News from everywhere, except, with disappointment for most of the crowd, there was little news of Estonia, Latvia Lithuania, the Ukraine or any of the other Soviet occupied countries from which many of us had fled. Nevertheless, this was very helpful to those who did not have anything in their language to read. Although our family was fluent in German, not all Estonians were. Uncle knew everyone's fate was very much determined by events far beyond our ability to control them. His program of news was of great value to everyone and for that he occupied a position of great respect at the DP camp.

Utmost on everyone's mind was the progress of the UNRRA, which had been formed in 1943 to address Europe's problem of what to do with over 6 million refugees as well as other post-war problems. Uncle Leonhard on this Friday evening in 1947 read to us that 2,326,000 of the 5,800,000 displaced persons in Germany had returned to their homelands. Today, he read, there are still 264,000 DPs in the British zone, 367,000 in the American zone and 26,000 in the French zone.

Mother and I knew already that while the numbers were staggering, many, like us, who refused to return to our homeland, were in a precarious position. What we cared about, sitting there listening to Uncle Leonhard, was whether the British would cave in to pressure by the Soviets to send us back. We knew this had been a mandate just after the war, that all citizens of Soviet occupied countries return to their homes. We had already refused. We knew Uncle Leonhard had also refused. We had been interviewed several times at Hannoversch-Münden and we repeated the story of the Soviet knock on our door long ago in Viivikond and Mother's period of hiding every time. How uneasy those interviews had been. Here we were, we were not brought to Germany as slave labor, something we learned the Nazis had done. We were not collaborators with the Nazi regime against the Soviets or against the Jews of Estonia. How do we explain that although we were not political people we would still be putting Mother's life in danger if we returned to our country? Yes, we preferred the Germans to the Russians. Not for political reasons, but because our very existence as educated people made us Soviet targets. Uncle's news could yield some progress for us and for everyone in that auditorium who was tired of living a life in transit. That is what life was. We were not settled in a permanent place. We were establishing schools and community but with the shared knowledge that all this was temporary and could be taken away from us with a simple policy change by the occupying powers.

We listened as Uncle shared the latest information about which countries were willing to take any number of the 6,795,000 civilians displaced by the war. From day to day, Mother and I considered Sweden, Britain, France, Canada, the United States, Australia – almost anywhere – but the negotiations reported in the newspaper did not reveal anything that we could depend upon for longer than a week at a time.

What caused me to sit up straight in my chair that evening was mention of something called the Displaced Persons Act, which was under debate in the United States. This policy, if enacted, would offer sanctuary to a limited number of refugees from communist countries. But this legislation was only in its formative stages that evening of Uncle's meeting. Yet this was the moment the idea lodged inside my mind...Mother and I will go to America. Europe, by the sound of things, would squabble about our fate forever. The economy in the United States was much better. Mother apparently agreed with me. She raised her hand and when Uncle recognized her, she said, "What is the likelihood that this will pass?"

He smiled. "I wish I had a crystal ball."

Afterwards, after many audience members stayed and discussed world events, we returned to Uncle's modest room to prepare for sleep, still discussing the news as we were laying out our blankets on the floor for sleeping. The next morning we were filled with energy. Mother and Uncle Leonhard were involved in a lengthy conversation, about something I wasn't giving any particular attention to when I heard a sharp knock on the door. I still responded with alert to mysterious knocks at the door even now in this safe place. Mother glanced at me and nodded so I turned and swung the door open wide. And, in the few brief silent seconds that followed, I took in the tall handsome man in a British naval uniform standing before me. Impeccably white, epaulets on each shoulder, shiny buttons and his hat tilted back so his bright eyes shone with his broad smile at the sight of me.

"Oh!" was all I could say.

Behind me, Mother and Uncle Leonhard had stopped talking. Then I heard my mother scream.

"Karli?"

For a brief moment it was as if a ghost were standing there before me. Mother stood up. Uncle Leonhard did too. Aunt Maanja and Helena watched us as we all cried out at once with a joy that words on a page simply cannot describe.

"You're...come in, come in." And Mother's arms were around her youngest brother she had not seen or heard from since he was taken with the ship he worked on to Leningrad in 1941. Uncle Leonhard wept. Karli embraced all of us, over and over again. What noise we must have made, disturbing everyone on our floor, with shouts of pleasure, a jumble of cries, words like "miracle, we thought you were dead, we were sure...Siberia...look at you...Oh my God!"

He was just as I remembered him. He, of course, couldn't believe it was me, sixteen years old; the last time he'd seen me I was nine.

The British Navy uniform was the ending of a long story. It was time for breakfast and work, but it hardly mattered. We sat and his first words explained how he found us. He expected to find Uncle Leonhard here, but certainly not Mother and me. He told us of searching list after list for the Vahter name finding Leonhard's name on a register of displaced persons in Lübeck, a harbor town in the north. He boarded a train to Hamburg then to Schwarzenbeck and here he was.

"Word from anyone else?" Of course that was our second question. He shook his head.

"Not yet," he said. Then he told us of his encounter with Artur in Leningrad in 1941 and how he had come across him by accident at the port there so long ago.

"We couldn't believe it," Karli said. "There we were, two brothers, and we both stood staring at each other like we were apparitions. Both of us were starving and looked like skeletons. I weighed less than one hundred pounds." He laughed, while I stared up at him, such a tall man at six feet, at least. "Tonight isn't the first time I've seen that expression on someone's face, Imbi."

Mother just kept squeezing his hand. Uncle tried to find some tea or coffee or something to serve, but quickly gave up. It was much more important to hear him tell us everything.

"They picked me up at the port in Tallinn," he said. "The Soviets left nobody who was young and strong. They put us all on the ship that I worked on and we arrived in Leningrad a few days later. We didn't know where we were going or what they'd do with us once we got there, but we suspected, even before we arrived, that we would be somewhere in Russia."

"They wanted to know what skills we had. I told them I was in the merchant marine. No use lying. I figured I'd end up in their navy or on a ship. And I did. I was on a ship that sat in the harbor at Leningrad while the city fell apart. The Germans cut off our food supplies. Ships couldn't go in or out. The city was starving. We were eating rats and mice we caught on the ship. If you found a cat you were in sheer luxury. I saw some people eating the bark of trees. The bombs were dropping every night. The Russians don't worry about their civilians. They took what food they could for the fighting men but I heard that they didn't have enough even for them. Nobody could leave Leningrad. They'd shoot you if you tried."

Uncle Leonhard said, "You look well fed now."

"You should have seen us," Karli said. "Skin and bones. I could have died there." His face changed slightly as he remembered some detail he wouldn't share with us.

"You didn't," Mother said, smiling through wet eyes. "How did you get out?"

"The Russian officer in charge of us on the ship came in one day. I need two volunteers," he said. Then, with a bland matter of fact tone, he said, "I knew I'd die if I didn't get out of there. I knew my chances were better if I at least did something, so I raised my hand. Turned out they wanted paratroopers."

"You jumped out of an airplane?" I asked.

"First they trained me. A Russian soldier named Slavik and I. He and I were given an assignment. They wanted us to parachute into Finland, into the forest. They had the place all picked out. Our job was to assassinate Mannerheim."

Uncle Karli with his wife Thea in Australia, 1952

Uncle Leonhard was quite astonished at this. "He was the leader of a neutral country!" he said.

"To the Soviets, if you are neutral you are the enemy since you are not helping." Karli's storytelling voice alternated between lighthearted and grim as he continued with his story.

"Mannerheim is still alive, isn't he?" Mother asked. "Did you go to Finland?" She looked at his uniform.

"Yes, they flew us over to Finland and dropped us. We landed deep in the woods. We were to find our way and figure out how to get near enough to kill him."

"They wanted you to commit murder..."

"Yes, but all I wanted was to get free – to escape from these lunatics."

"But you were with a Russian soldier. Wouldn't he turn you in if you didn't follow orders?"

"You would think so. But who could he turn me in to in Finland? He would more likely shoot me." He paused. "How do I say this? Slavik was on the verge of starvation too. But I was ready to kill *him* if he interfered with my plans. I knew it would have to be that way. I was not going to take part in this crazy plan. I'd be killed. Mannerheim was so well protected. I knew I'd never get near him."

We all sat, waiting for him to continue. He saw our faces. Here he was, alive, sitting before us. The dread of hearing what he'd tell us next was in our eyes.

"So here we were, in this field in the dark. Slavik looked at me. I stared back at him. We both had weapons. Then I saw it in his face. He had no intention of trying to carry out this ridiculous mission either. And he was prepared to kill me too, if I got in his way." Karli responded to the relief on our faces. "He saw the same thing in me. So, no, I did not have to kill him. Slavik said to me, 'So, shall we go turn ourselves in to the Finnish authorities? Perhaps they will give us something to eat'." Karli laughed. "And that is what we did, together."

"Next, the Finns interrogated us and we told them as much as we knew. They wanted to use us. They sent us back behind Russian lines with communication equipment and we intercepted Russian communication signals and reported what we could back to the Finnish authorities. We were dropped again by parachute. I still am not sure exactly where we were. Of course, we worried that they would abandon us on Russian soil, but they didn't. They came back for us."

"But this is a British uniform," I said.

"I'm not finished Imbi," my uncle said. "After we were back in Finland we were given our freedom."

So Uncle Karli left Finland to seek political asylum in Sweden and it was granted to him, but the Swedes were under pressure by the Soviet Union to return all refugees to their country of origin, including Estonians. Uncle Karli had learned that those sent back to Estonia disappeared and were not heard from ever again. This, he knew, was not the path for him. So he and sixteen other men organized a small boat and sailed it to England.

"We were put in jail when we arrived," Uncle Karli said with a smile. "We had no papers. But at least in England we were fed and we were safe."

When the British heard Uncle's story, it took them six months to release him, but not before investigating his background to verify his story. He did not know the fate of the other fifteen men he sailed with.

Uncle Karli joined the Royal Navy and sailed to Germany and here he was. Of course, what we desired the most was to somehow get word that he was alive back to Grandmother Olga at home. The border was closed, and he could be in danger if the Soviets knew of his betrayal and defection. A letter would surely be opened and read by the authorities of what was now a police state. But, for that day, it was a joy to sit with him and rejoice that he was alive, healthy and that he had found us.

Uncle Karli didn't stay with us long. He was due back on his ship that evening. In his subsequent travels, he saw the Middle East, Australia and most of the world. He worked his way up to be the captain on a transport ship. He married a young Estonian woman, Thea Silvere, in Australia and had three daughters.

Mother and I returned to Göttingen and our usual routines. Information fluctuated daily. Everyone, down to the last person at our camp wanted to find a place to make a permanent home. The occupying forces, through diplomatic channels, changed the reported status of possible host countries that would allow Estonian citizens in exile into their country and allow them to gain legal residency status. And, as we waited for some sign of what might be our best next step, Uncle Karli's story warned us. If we stayed in Europe, pressure from the ever more powerful Soviet Union to return citizens to eastern lands like ours could win out no matter how many times we pleaded our case with our host country. Yes, we both agreed, the United States or even Australia would be our safest options. But how we could make this happen or, even if we could find a way to make it happen, what would it take and how long would we have to wait?

CHAPTER 25

We lived in Göttingen until summer of 1948 at which time we and many other families from all over the British Zone were transferred to Lingen, a place near the River Ems up north near the Netherlands. This camp was created especially for families with school-age children. There we made new friendships that have lasted a lifetime. School was intense as ever, but always well balanced with sports and dancing.

Rumors began to circulate that several countries were willing to accept some refugees. Everybody stormed the application desk at the first opportunity, although only a small number were accepted each time. For many of us it was a disappointment to be rejected, but there was always hope for more openings. Refugees were moved to a series of transit camps as the world began to shift, to feel stable, and we began, along with so many other displaced persons, to visualize with more probability and hope, a return to a normal life with a home and a means to earn a living. At the transit camps, we were subject to very thorough investigations. We filled out piles and piles of papers answering questions about our lives during the war. Where had we lived? What work had we done? Names of persons we worked for or with, any means by which the British occupiers and their allies could corroborate our identities and our stories. What were our political views? Questions about our family members, their fate, their current whereabouts, their political beliefs, actions during the occupations, military service, education – so many questions. Then, we went to interviews with nameless men in uniforms. We knew about the Nuremberg Trials for war criminals. The crimes against fellow human beings by Nazis had surfaced and the victors set themselves to punish criminals among the German people and collaborators in any German occupied countries. No host country wanted war criminals settling within their borders. I thought of our landlady in Wolfenbüttel and how she snooped in our room and the distrust and how it led to my arrest for my ration coupons. I couldn't help but wonder if she did that to hide something about herself. Imagine, being refused entry to a country because of my little crime with my double ration coupons!

Increasingly, our fellow displaced persons found countries to accept them. Many went to whatever country was open to accepting Estonians at the time. Silently, we were wishing to go to America. Mother and I waited. Refugees left almost daily to Canada, Australia, Britain, the United States and to many other places. We waved goodbye to DP camp friends and neighbors who had become like family to us. So many here, so many there. The following week, perhaps the numbers changed and all of a sudden several hundred persons shipped out without warning. Mother and I waited. In early 1948 we knew no one in the

United States. To be allowed to enter, we needed a sponsor, a church, a citizen, who would guarantee us a place to live and a job. Mother and I knew that unless the rules changed we just might not get there.

Aunt Maanja's sister Helena was one of the first accepted by England. She left Uncle Leonhard and Aunt Maanja in 1948 and became one of England's White Swans, women who worked in their hospitals attending their war wounded. She chose to stay in England once she settled there. We learned of this in our correspondence with Uncle Leonhard.

Once again Uncle Leonhard came to our rescue. His wife Maanja had kept up a correspondence with someone from her school days in Estonia. This woman, Elisabeth Smith, emigrated to the United States, married and lived on Kings Highway, Brooklyn, New York. She responded to Aunt Maanja's letter and agreed to host Leonhard and Maanja in her home and to help them to find jobs. So, two years after that fortunate and amazingly memorable Friday with Uncle Karli in 1946, Uncle Leonhard and Aunt Maanja sailed to America. This was all well and good for them, but Mother and I were left behind. We received a letter several weeks later from Uncle letting us know they arrived and that Elisabeth's house was very comfortable but quite small. They lived in one of the three bedrooms. His first order of business, after finding himself a job, he promised, was to find a way to clear the path for Mother and me to join them.

The saving grace during this period was the exchange of letters between Mother and Leonhard who encouraged us and gave us hope. His plan was to liberate himself by earning his United States citizenship. But, this was a five year-process. Only then, he wrote, could he sponsor us but that would be far in the future. Elisabeth, being a kind and compassionate person, also promised to take us in when the time came.

Waiting was not unusual. We'd been waiting and hoping with great patience for so long, for life to resume what we knew was its natural state, despite not having experienced what you might call a 'normal' existence since long before the first Soviet invasion. So we kept up with school, both of us, and watched as our neighbors packed what little they had and departed for transit camps after hugs and kisses and promises to write. What, I wondered, as I kissed yet another schoolmate farewell, would happen to their letters addressed to us here if we were no longer here? Would the DP camp forward mail? Each day there was less and less for us here in Germany. We received CARE packages occasionally from the American Red Cross and the International Red Cross. Still, we were a burden on this ruined country. Rebuilding had started, but it wasn't only the physical Germany that needed reconstruction. The German people still struggled with their ruined economy, their railways and highways in need of repair, the rubble of bombed cities in need of reconstruction. Neighbors had betrayed neighbors and many had learned of the death of former friends. The distrust of friends and the fear of recrimination due to misplaced loyalty to the National Socialist Party put everyone on the defensive. Having obeyed orders in the service of a country at war could mean you'd broken international law and you could be sentenced by the Allies who held trials and hunted for former members of the SS. The newspapers kept us informed. While much of this did not touch us personally it still set an uneasy climate for Germans and Ausländen. We would follow Uncle Leonhard and Aunt Maanja and we would leave this behind us...it would happen, we just couldn't say when.

Finally, we heard from Uncle Leonhard. He had gotten a job at Mount Sinai hospital in New York City as a letter carrier and he and Aunt Maanja were settled in their own apartment. Elisabeth would give us a roof over our heads and act as our sponsor.

Each day, along with many others, we waited for the administrators to make announcements for us to go to Wentorf Transit Camp. I checked and double-checked our status. I first had to be sure that the officials had updated our records to show that Elisabeth was our sponsor. We were transported to transit camp and one week later to Bremerhaven to board a ship to the United States. After months we surged with hope. There it was, Mother's name, Lydia Vahter. She was assigned to leave the following day on an American transport ship. I was ecstatic only for a brief moment, because, it soon was clear that Mother was listed, but my name was not on the list. Up to the front of the crowd I went and elbowed my way to the desk.

"Excuse me," I said. "But my mother is on this list for America. And my name is not."

"What is your name?" asked the white haired man with a handlebar mustache and a tight uniform with buttons straining against the buttonholes. "Imbi Peebo," I responded. "I am her daughter."

"What? The names are not the same." I felt a touch of impatience. How many questions had we answered? How many times had we explained?

It was a bright day in January, with a sky so deeply blue over the water where I heard the gulls cry and flap their wings against a strong westward wind. I checked my impatience and said it again. "My parents are divorced," I said. "Mine is my father's name."

"Is he here?" his eyes scanned the list.

"No." I braced myself for more questions. "He is not here. I believe he is still in Estonia." Silently I prayed he was, and he and Elsa and Taavet were together where I'd last seen them. "Only my mother and I escaped."

"You cannot go. There is only room for her." He frowned at me.

"She will not go then." I knew there was always a wait list in case someone became ill or chose not to go. "Let someone else on."

"Tsk," he emitted this through a prim set of lips. Then he looked up. "Alright then," he said. "Come back and check with us again tomorrow."

This went on and on for weeks. My name would get assigned to a ship and Mother's would not. Or, she would be assigned again without me. There was always a wait list. If someone was ill they could not get on a ship. So, the authorities kept a list and if someone dropped off the passenger list, the next person would be allowed on.

We were terribly frustrated. I felt like we would never leave, never have that final green light. Finally, after I watched one more friend, our dear Aino, who was practically a sister, step aboard an American ship and wave goodbye, I made my way back to the transport office. I had no cigarettes to bribe someone with. I was powerless, but I was my father's daughter, and I took charge.

I asked to see the top ranking official. I stood and refused to take no for an answer. I insisted, and said I was willing to wait all day if necessary. You see, I had already waited for so long, this didn't upset me. Finally, late in the afternoon, I was allowed to see the man in charge. I do not remember his name or what he looked like. By this time I had encountered so many English-speaking men in uniform, in my memory they all are a big blur.

"My mother and I must be assigned on the same ship," I stated in my firmest voice. Then, when he responded that of course families were to travel together and to the same place, I exploded. "My mother and I have different last names. She is Vahter. I am Peebo. Mine is my father's name. They divorced when I was five years old." I had said this so often, but this time I said it with such desperate frustration I had to remind myself to not show anger. "We have been waiting and repeating this for weeks. Please mark your records to put us together."

He sat up straight and rigid in his chair and for an instant, I feared I had stepped over the line and he would refuse me. Behind my worry was a strong recollection of my father's words, "Imbi, you are in charge of the family," and I felt a cool confidence wash over and through me. I took a deep breath and smiled at him, a weak, apologetic smile. "I cannot leave my mother alone," I said.

"And," he said in return, "She would never leave a child, would she?"

I shook my head no.

"Let me see," he lowered his eyes to his desk. Our records were there in a neat folder. I forced myself to sit quietly and resisted the urge to recite for him the many times my mother or I took one or the other of us off the departure list and allowed someone to go in our place.

"How old are you?" he glanced up for a second.

"Seventeen," I said.

"Almost an adult, really," he said.

With surprise I realized he was right. I was still physically small, barely five feet one inch. I hadn't grown for several years and now it occurred to me that I was almost an adult and this put a bit of worry in me.

"You are old enough to travel alone," he said. "We could send her and we can get you on the next one."

"We go together, or we don't go," I said.

He sat up even taller. I half expected him to stand up and lean over his huge desk at me.

"Young lady," he said. "Who is in charge here, you or me?"

I stared at him. He stared back. I stood up from the stiff chair I'd been occupying while he scrutinized our papers. I put my two hands on his desk and leaned in until my eyes were level with his. I smiled although I was not feeling very friendly, but he couldn't know that. He leaned back in his chair, his eyes fixed on me. "Sir," I said, "It is my life. And it is my mother's life. We are inseparable. You are here to help displaced persons find a new place to live and start over, yes?"

"Yes," he said. "And you are one of perhaps thousands of people who need our help."

"Do you know why I need your help and why I can't go back to Estonia and why I can't be separated from my mother?"

"I read your files. Yes, I understand they were looking for your mother."

"Yes, and after she managed to get away and come back to me, after months of hiding, she and I swore we would never be separated again, except if one of us died."

He studied his desktop.

"You don't want me to break that promise, do you? When I was five years old, my father told me I was in charge of the family. I am. You are not in charge of my family, I am. And I say that my mother and I must go on the same ship or not go at all."

"How could he say that to a five year old?"

"I don't know. I didn't know then why he said it, or how to be in charge of the family. But, I am seventeen now and I still remember that he said it and now that I am an adult, I can be in charge. So I will not stay without my mother and she will not go without me." I sat back down. "Do you know how many times we have passed up a passage because it was for only one of us?"

"Are you both sure you want to leave Germany? You've turned down at least a dozen opportunities to go."

"We have a sponsor in the United States. We have relatives there. Is someone blocking our departure deliberately?"

"Why would anyone do that?"

"I don't know. Except that the Russians are your allies and perhaps they don't want you to let us go."

"Why you? You and your mother are not that important to them."

"Then what is the problem? Why is nobody putting us together on a ship?

He folded his hands and looked over them at me. "Imbi," he said, "I don't know why you haven't been given passage on the same ship, but I will put you on the waiting list for this ship this time. If anyone cancels or becomes ill, you'll get on."

"How long is the wait list now?" I asked feeling a sense of victory but a limited one.

"You are number eighteen," he said.

"Is that the best you can do?"

"Yes."

"If I don't get on, Mother will not go either."

"We'll see. It is a chance; a small chance, but I'm trying, young lady."

I stood up. "Okay, the ship leaves in three days? I will watch the wait list, thank you."

And so Mother and I packed, and I checked the list daily. Slowly, over the next few days, my name inched up the list. From eighteenth, to sixteenth, to thirteenth. And it held there for a full 24 hours. Then, as we began to consider withdrawing entirely, a family of seven withdrew and I was suddenly number six. Then, the ship's departure was delayed for a day. We were about to give up again, resigned to another visit to the transit office to beg for both of us to only be put on lists together when another group of six people came down with the flu and were withdrawn. Suddenly, we knew! We were both on! The time had come.

We were elated, scared, uncertain, but thrilled to finally have this path opened for us. Mother sent a telegram to Uncle Leonhard in New York. It said simply, "We arrive on General Muir on 20 January, 1950."

The departure was scheduled for noon. We were to report to the ship by nine a.m. with whatever belongings we could fit in the allotted amount of bags. That was not a problem because we still had so little to carry. We bid farewell to friends who'd been our substitute family and of course, thought of those back home who we could not bid goodbye. We found our berth on the ship, a high room near the bow with bunk beds. We didn't care how tight our accommodations were, we were accustomed to anything.

Mother and I walked aboard together, side by side, and as I stepped up the gangplank, I passed by the officer who had found me that place on the waiting list. I stopped. "Thank you," I said.

"Good luck," he said in reply. He looked for a moment at my mother. "Remember who is in charge," he said to her.

"My daughter has been in charge since birth," Mother said with a laugh. "I'm glad you understood."

As the ship sounded its horn and moved slowly through the harbor and into the stormy English Channel, we realized we were no longer in Germany. We were headed out across the huge Atlantic Ocean. Mother and I had a choice. We could stay on the eastern deck and wave goodbye to the country we'd lived in for five years since the end of the war, the place we'd spent the most time living since my birth seventeen years earlier. We could stand there and look back, across years to our summers at the farm, our vacations at Narva Jõesuu, to Narva and the garden with one hundred and forty two gooseberry bushes and a looming Russian church. We could. Or, we could push our way to the western facing deck and look into our future, and all the new adventures that lay waiting for us. I chose and Mother followed me, at the bow of our ship, facing into the blue waters and setting sun looking forward to the unknown that lay ahead, sure that no matter what came next, and no matter who was in charge, we would face it together and we would make good of whatever our new home country held for us for the rest of our lives.

Epilogue

*Imbi's story does not end here. But this is a good place to close up this account of her early years. Her experiences as a child in what Tom Snyder calls **The Bloodlands**, in his book of the same name, are representative of many others who grew up in Europe during this time in history. Many stories have been told but only now that the Soviets no longer control the fifteen republics they annexed as part of their aggressive imperialist attempt to take over much of the free world, now that these countries are independent, these stories of emigrants cannot hurt the families left behind in Soviet police states. The stories long hidden can now be shared with the world.*

Imbi attended a reading of this book in progress at Montclair State University where I teach. She brought along her two children Reino and Sirike. Her daughter confided in me afterwards that her mother's personal Estonian history lessons were the subject of conversation at the dinner table through much of her childhood. She smiled and said she knows so much of her mother's story, but because the dinnertime telling of it left much of its timeline uncertain, it was wonderful to see someone organizing the episodes that were so familiar into a narrative. I was grateful for the support of Imbi's children in this effort. Reino had confided in me earlier that his interest was for his own children who didn't sit through all those dinners with Imbi and her mother Lydia.

I confessed to Imbi's children my sense of my own limitations as narrator for this story. I can't recall all the daily details, the food they ate, the shortages of food staples and materials for life, the rituals of everyday and the harsh interruptions to quotidian life. But, while I knew I could not give this story all that it needs, I somehow could visualize the farm, the village, the pine forest, and the sense of vulnerability Imbi and her family experienced. As I moved through each episode, there were places and events that came alive to me as she talked. I can see the farm and the sauna. I can hear the birds in the trees and the trickle of the river that ran through the family farm in Lauraveski, near Mahu. I can hear her laughter with her cousins as they go about the daily maintenance of life on a humble farm near the Gulf of Finland.

As I write this, I hear Imbi with the innocence of a child as she recalls her childhood. I also hear Imbi, the mature woman, a grandmother, and an accomplished scientist whose career in the United States was as remarkable as her years of flight in Estonia, Poland and Germany. And, inevitably, I hear her reflection on the history of World War II and its impact on the personal lives of so many courageous people and particularly the Vahter family and the Peebo family, Imbi's relatives who each faced variations of oppression whether they stayed in Estonia or fled. Only she really knew how hard fought that battle for survival was until this telling of her story.

Stalin killed far more innocent people than did Hitler. Imbi's story of her childhood tells us that when you are struggling for survival in such a situation, especially if you are a child, you simply do not know of such things as concentration camps, gas chambers, death squads. The news media in any occupied country is controlled by the occupiers during wartime. They tell you whatever serves their cause, and nothing else. They certainly didn't let ordinary people know of the atrocities they committed. Imbi, like so many others, learned much later of such things.

As Imbi came of age, her awareness began to take shape at Treptow when she stumbled upon the graveyard of the mentally ill and learned they'd died at the hands of their own government. That, on top of her experience of the continued war, the destruction of so many cities and the loss of so many lives at the hands of warring nations are indelibly etched on her memory. The full emotional impact of this recognition can be illustrated in the story with which I end this book.

Imbi and Arvid Truumees made many trips back to Europe in their adult lives. Many of these trips included visits to the places they remember from childhood, to see for themselves the changes history brought and also to teach their children of the places and people of their past, to visit relatives, to bring them goods from the west unavailable in Estonia under the rule of the Soviets, but also to add to their knowledge of history to fill in the gaps of information about what they had lived through, what they'd experienced as children.

In 2001, Imbi and Arvid visited Germany and Austria. While there, they made a purposeful visit to Auschwitz, to the memorial to the Jews who lost their lives at the German concentration and extermination camps of the Nazi era. Imbi toured Auschwitz with a busload of travelers in search of history. As she walked through this museum, she saw the place where so many were brutally murdered, and the harsh conditions for those who labored as prisoners of the Nazis. Gas chambers, barracks, latrines, mass graves. At the end of the tour, she saw the room full of shoes, children's shoes, shoes filling up a room to the ceiling...all shoes that had once belonged to the children who were sent here, who labored here and were put to death here. These children had been her age. She became so overwhelmed, so upset at the sight of this, she said to Arvid, "I will meet you on the bus." And she left. She reflects, as she tells me this episode of horror.

All I could think about was that they were children just like I was a child during that time. Those shoes. All belonging to children. Children who were killed, just killed for being in the way of a madman."

Arvid and I left the museum. We got on the bus to sit by ourselves and wait. I was hiding the tears I could not stop from streaming down my face. The bus driver and our tour guide were listening to the radio. The guide turned to me and said, "Are you American?"

I nodded.

"Someone just flew a jet into the World Trade Center," he said. He turned up the radio. And I listened to the report of the second plane when it flew into the second tower. Here we were, so far away, hearing of this going on in the country we had fled to, where we found peace and freedom and a life of family and friends, prosperity and opportunity. And my feeling was so full of fright right there with all the sadness of the past of which I had just been reminded. "Will we ever stop killing each other?" I asked the guide.

So many years after Mother and I had escaped the terror of a police state, I keep repeating the same question, "Will we ever stop?"